A Master Surgeon of the Heart

A Master Surgeon of the Heart

DAVID EDMONSTON

Epigraph Books
Rhinebeck, New York

A Master Surgeon of the Heart © Copyright 2023 by David Edmonston

All rights reserved. No part of this book may be used or reproduced in any manner without the consent of the author except in critical articles or reviews. Contact the publisher for information.

Paperback ISBN 978-1-960090-22-5
eBook ISBN 978-1-960090-23-2

Library of Congress Control Number 2023912856

Cover art by Steve Kuzma, artofkuzma@gmail.com
Book design by Colin Rolfe

Epigraph Books
22 East Market Street, Suite 304
Rhinebeck, New York 12572
(845) 876-4861
epigraphps.com

You are in the hands of a Master Surgeon of the heart.
This is open-heart surgery.
It is that serious and that wonderful.
When the operation is over, there will be no scar,
and the cure will be so complete that
no one will even remember the sickness.

—WORDS OF AN INNER VOICE
SPOKEN TO THE WRITER (CHAPTER 15)

To the Reader

I've been involved in a spiritual study for over half a century. I'm a slow and skeptical learner, often refusing to accept the words of my teachers until repeated life experiences have verified for me what they say. What I've learned is of great value to me and might also be of value to others, so I've felt it necessary to report my learning experiences truthfully. It would be against my nature to tell another person what to believe. But I would encourage everyone to seek their own spiritual experiences.

This isn't a near-death experience story. I haven't visited the other side, nor have I suffered the trauma often associated with such an experience. But I have explored the meaning of life and how life is more accurately perceived from the perspective of a higher plane, as many near-death experiencers have likewise concluded. That exploration I needed to do for myself. My exploration is far from finished, but I feel a need to give a report of highlights from my journey so far.

Many people helped me in preparing this book. This memoir had its beginning in the 1990s, when my friend Bruno Zaffina said to a small group of fellow spiritual aspirants, "We should collect the stories of the experiences of the initiates. They will be valuable in future times." I told him that I had begun writing some of my own stories, and that his encouragement would keep me writing. As my collection of stories grew around the turn of the millennium, I wished to make it presentable to others. Then Barry Lerner and Sheila Rogers DeMare gave me extensive help with editing. My wife, Heidi, kept finding and questioning statements I'd made that needed explanation or support. And still the collection of stories slowly grew. More recently, my son, Steven, has asked many questions, helping me to identify passages needing clarification. Throughout the writing project, David Newcomb has been a one-man cheering section, encouraging me to believe that this project was a worthwhile service. While preparing this memoir for its present publication, now unified under the theme of my spiritual education, a number of friends have helped by reading and critiquing the text. They are: Gerry Gorman, Carolyn Khanna, Arran Stephens, David Newcomb, James Delsie, Katie Hodari, Andrew Vidich, and especially Barry Lerner (again), who gave me extensive, professional editing suggestions and advice as a gift from his own generous heart.

The inspired artist, Steve Kuzma, beautifully expressed the mood of my vision of the tall ship (chapter 1) for the cover illustration. That illustration is actually a re-envisioning of my earlier vision. The background, with the ship, is what the vision showed to me, but I asked the artist to include the person having the vision in the foreground of the picture. And instead of that person turned to view the vision, I asked that he be turned forward, looking and gesturing toward the observer of the picture. That's because, over many years, I've changed from one simply being shown a vision to one who is now also challenged with expressing the spiritual vision to others—even though I'm still a beginner on the spiritual path and have only the meager pallet of words with which to communicate.

This book grew out of the lifetime of learning inspired by my three spiritual teachers, Sant Kirpal Singh Ji (1894 – 1974), Sant Darshan Singh Ji (1921 – 1989), and Sant Rajinder Singh Ji (b. 1946), who have taught me everything I was capable of learning so far about spirituality. Although the words of my spiritual teachers have been quoted in many places, this isn't a full explanation of their teachings; rather it's an account of how I came to my own partial understanding of those teachings with confirmations through my own life experiences. I've had a great deal of help from those spiritual teachers that was given to me out of simple love. I've been taught with gentleness and respect, and sometimes, as will be seen, with a keen sense of drama. If critical readers challenge my interpretations of my experiences, to them I would say, "Learning is always a tentative process. Still, those experiences that have touched my soul do have, for me, the fragrance of truth, of reality."

Above all, there is that divine Power overhead, which has been a motive force and writing partner throughout the many years since this writing project began. While I may put my name on the book, and readers might think that I conceived it all, I am in wonder over the inner help and many suggestions made by this selfless writing partner, who, I think, has more right of authorship than I do.

For more information about the spiritual teachings described here, I recommend the website of Science of Spirituality: sos.org.

DAVID EDMONSTON,
APRIL 26, 2023,
BOWLING GREEN, VIRGINIA, USA

Contents

PART 1
Years of Seeking

CHAPTER ONE

Premonition

1959

A shadow lay over my life throughout my childhood and teen years. I had lost something that I couldn't name or describe. It wasn't anything of this world but was terribly important. Then, when I was seventeen, a vision came that assured me that there was good hope of regaining what was lost. I was sitting at my desk, reading, while listening to Brahms' Piano Concerto No. 1. In the music, I heard a passage for French horns that moved me to tears. I felt that the music spoke of that very thing I had lost. I sobbed with longing.

Then, I was no longer aware of my room or my desk. I was standing atop a cliff, facing a body of water, a fjord, a small bay surrounded by stony cliffs. The water was sparkling in golden sunlight. On the water was a tall ship with square sails curved out with wind behind them. It was coming to take me aboard with other people, to carry us to that mysterious thing that I had lost, that we *all* had lost. I still heard the music of the French horns, now coming from the ship, echoing off the cliffs. I was being called, and my heart said "Yes!" A short time later the horn passage ended, and I was sitting at my desk again, still weeping with longing and gratitude. The vision was over.

Since then, throughout my life, when I hear the same music, or even speak of that experience, the picture of that ship is clear in my mind and the sweet, heart-wrenching longing of the vision and the music overpowers my heart again. Today, I am eighty years old, seeing life with a little distance, and I can now interpret that vision as a premonition—perhaps a promise—that in time the means to fulfill a deeply felt need that was then beyond my understanding would come my way.

I'm convinced that we humans come into this life for a purpose. That purpose is our inner growth. That growth can take many forms, such as growth of understanding, growth of character, growth of consciousness, or growth of our identity. If we are not making progress in that purpose, then we feel restless, unhappy, just as I felt before my vision. I was like so many others, caught in the materialism of Western culture. I was blind to my own spiritual identity. That was the thing I had lost. I knew nothing about who and what I was. I wasn't progressing as I needed to. And, as a young adult, every material life goal or career that I examined seemed hollow and depressing, without hope of fulfillment. But visions don't come without a purpose behind them, and a vision had come. Hope returned.

Guru Nanak, the first of the ten Sikh Gurus, said:

> *The ship, being non-material, needs no air and water,*
> *It is the Boat of Naam that takes one to the other side.*[1]

At the time of that vision I knew nothing about Guru Nanak, nor about his allegorical "Boat of Naam." That nautical imagery came to my vision spontaneously. Surely, it was the "Boat of Naam" that had manifested in my vision. It would be eight years before this vision would have definite meaning for me. In the meantime, I had to go through a long period of searching—not knowing what I was searching for—at first, without even knowing that I *was* searching. Then, metaphorically speaking, I boarded that ship fifty-six years ago, in 1967, when I was initiated by Sant Kirpal Singh Ji of India. I haven't yet reached my destination. I'm still aboard that ship, moving gradually toward my goal. But some incidents in the voyage so far have been quite interesting. I'd like to share them with you. I'll tell of life-changing experiences with my spiritual teachers, of my inner longings, fears, understandings, and spiritual visions. I'll describe how I was taught and how I learned. This is a memoir mostly about how I began to learn of the inner side—the spiritual side—of human beings, especially of myself. I'm telling this story truthfully, so truthfully that, as I begin this account, I feel quite exposed.

When my search began, without understanding,
Seeking for wisdom to grasp at life's mysteries
Amid teachers and students blind to deep meaning—
"It's wrong to seek truth amid spiritual things,
The world of matter is all that there is.
The purpose of life is for wealth and for pleasure,
For pride in discovery of what can be used.
To seek in the non-material realm
Is just waste of time. Stay with the real!"
The world spoke strongly. Where shall I seek?

CHAPTER TWO

Awakening

1961–1964

On a sunny day in September 1961, I sat beside a stream in a wooded park, reading a textbook for my first college course in philosophy. When I closed my book, the sun shone warmly through the canopy of leaves high overhead. The world that I saw then was not the normal world that I knew but was suffused with golden light. It seemed that the secret wonders of nature had become visible. With newly awakened vision I could see the joyous and fearful drama of the power of life and the rightful function of death in nature. Even the rocks and the water seemed to be conscious partners in the dance of life. It was a serious, a solemn experience. I thought that while I had been reading, the world had changed, becoming more beautiful, richer, deeper, more alive. Captivated, I stood and reverently walked on the gravel beside the stream. I reached out to nearby tree branches and gently pressed the living leaves to my face. I leaned down and touched my fingertips to the conscious water. I felt so awake and so happy.

Perhaps time was passing in the world outside this place of golden light. Yet I was reluctant to leave. I thought I would lose the wonder I'd just experienced. As I rode my bicycle out of the park, the world I saw around me became drab and flat, as usual. I grieved for my loss and resolved to return to that stream another day to renew my vision.

Weeks later, I did return to the stream in the park. I waited expectantly, but the experience of the magic in nature didn't return. I asked, "How could it be that this special place won't show itself?" I stood still and wrestled with that question. Then I became aware that the whole world might be constantly overflowing with that magic, while my mind was closed to its wonder. If that were true, then the conscious change had been in my own awareness; it was not something in this park that had changed. That must be the answer. And here I was, expecting the world to change but not myself!

If my understanding were true, then such experiences might be had anywhere. I began to ask how I might grow so my life would be woven with more experiences of such consciousness. For the first time, an understanding of the age-old questions of truth, consciousness, and love became imperative to me. Before, I had played with those concepts for intellectual entertainment, but now I saw them as absolutely fundamental to a satisfactory life. I felt a new fear: that I might be unable to address them. I was nineteen years old. I had read some philosophy. I knew how frustrated even wise philosophers were over their own limitations of understanding. But now I also knew that like many other people, I *must* try to answer those questions with solid, personal experiences and find the missing consciousness, even if it took a lifetime. All this passed through my mind while I stood by that stream, wishing for a conscious vision, which did not come.

THE PEACE MOVEMENT

My parents gave me a liberal religious upbringing, exposing me to many ways of thinking, while not imposing or forbidding any religious teaching or philosophy. My father, a mathematician, spent many evenings with me, sharing his own thoughts and by his example teaching me an appreciation for rational thought and expression. I thought of myself as non-religious, or as a humanist: one who is agnostic toward the divine, but sees and respects the great wonder of human life. That orientation of skepticism toward formal religions, along with a profound respect for humanity, and a search for greater consciousness, has only deepened throughout my life-long spiritual quest. As the story of my quest began, I was turning my attention away from the home of my loving parents, wanting to begin shaping my own life and thoughts. But one new influence came to me right at home.

My uncle, Henry Dyer, a Quaker, often visited with my family while attending political demonstrations in nearby Washington, DC, to protest America's part in developing and stockpiling nuclear weapons. In the late 1950s and early 60s, during the period of the "arms race," anyone advocating *fewer* weapons seemed to me like someone trying to hold back a freight train by hand. My mother, his sister, told me that during World War II he had been a conscientious objector to war, embracing the sacredness of life. This kindly, soft-spoken man had been imprisoned for refusing the draft. In prison, he went on a hunger strike. The prison officials, fearing that he might die in their custody, had him tied up and force-fed with a tube. My mother told me that, although he was still a young man when he was released from prison many months later, his dark hair had turned white, suggesting the stress he had endured. Because of his protests, and those of many others, a new law eventually was passed recognizing conscientious objectors and providing them some alternatives to combat duty. My parents didn't share my uncle's political perspective, but they respected his sincerity and courage. I could see that he could think for himself and followed his conscience even in the face of severe adversity.

I was a little afraid to ask him about his underlying beliefs—afraid, perhaps, of where the question might lead me.

Still, one evening I asked Uncle Henry how he had come to embrace the views he had. He promised to write to me about it. A few weeks later he sent a short letter and a booklet that explained the Quaker position on social and political conflicts. The booklet was *Speak Truth to Power.*[2] It described some of the ways, other than through violence, in which Quakers have dealt with social conflicts. There was a clarity and simplicity in this writing that invited understanding on a deeper level than anything I had previously read. It spoke of human beings as spiritual entities, each with a heart and with social value. This perspective resonated with me, even if I didn't have the experience to fully understand it. Soon I, too, became active in the peace movement, and I sometimes joined student- or Quaker-led demonstrations for disarmament in front of the White House.

I felt that only a society that took social fairness seriously could remain at peace. So I also became active in the civil rights movement. In August 1963, I attended the March on Washington, at which Martin Luther King Jr. gave his now famous *I Have a Dream* speech at the Lincoln Memorial. I still remember the intensity of Dr. King's voice. His vision of human unity was so powerful that I could practically see the social changes to come. As part of that huge crowd I felt I was participating in the growth of human consciousness.

WITH QUAKERS AT EARLHAM COLLEGE

I began college at Montgomery Community College in Maryland. That was a good experience. Often, after lectures, a handful of students would gather around the professor to discuss his ideas further. Frequently, I was one of them. Significantly, one teacher taught me to think of the word "truth" not as a noun—not as a thing—but as an adjective, as "truthful" in a classic sense: truth to an ideal. That concept has served me well throughout life. There, I grew personally and academically, but I still didn't find the deep understanding I was seeking.

Because of my interest in the peace movement, I next enrolled in a Quaker college, Earlham College, in Indiana. While there (from September 1963 to June 1964) I read about the history of the Quakers, a Christian sect that grew out of the mystic experiences of a small group of people in England in 1652. That made me wonder if the experiences of the mystics could shed light on my questions about life and consciousness, but I met no one at Earlham who could teach me more about that—with the exception of one professor, of whom I will speak shortly.

At Earlham College, I studied both chemistry and philosophy. Chemistry attracted me because I had enjoyed a first college course in chemistry. Philosophy attracted me because I had been told that the questions I was asking were the questions of philosophy, so in philosophy I hoped to find not just questions but answers. So far, I had read some writers who sounded wise, perhaps, but after my studies of them I felt no wiser myself. I had not yet abandoned this study, although eventually I concluded that the only wisdom to be found there was the knowledge of my own ignorance, which was something indeed, but it didn't address my crying need for growth in understanding, love, and consciousness.

During that fall and winter the experience of consciousness that I had found while sitting in the park teased me, not returning, but not leaving me alone. I felt I *must* pursue this consciousness. I wanted to recapture the experience of awakening, but I didn't have an inkling of how to do it, and I didn't know where to turn for help or even what questions to ask. Trying to succeed academically, I stayed up late at night to study, but my desire for consciousness and understanding forced itself uppermost in my mind. Soon, I couldn't concentrate on my coursework. Once, in frustration, I asked my academic adviser to help me figure out what, in my mind, was drawing me away from my coursework. He asked me, "What is it you most want?"

After thinking, I answered, "I want to *understand.*"

Ignoring my answer, he restated his question: "Do you want to become a chemist, or a philosopher?" I still studied both these fields, unable to settle on a major, but that was not my question then. I needed to know what *else* I was so interested in without being able to name it or describe it. That was when I realized that this professor would not—probably *could* not—answer my question. He was trying to help, but I felt he didn't *understand* at all. He was a philosophy professor—I had thought that of all my professors he would share my need for understanding and would know how to pursue it. But I was asking for something that he might have considered unrealistic or impractical to pursue. After that, I nearly despaired of ever finding a teacher with the understanding or wisdom that I needed.

I went for long walks alone, sometimes late at night in a park-like cemetery near the college. I felt I was somehow being led, and I was impatient to follow, but I didn't know what I must do. My inability to address my inner need made me very anxious. Although I was usually a buoyant person, during that winter I had several periods of depression. One winter night, walking alone, I crossed a footbridge over a stream. Looking down, I noticed how the water flowed, so fluidly, so serenely, in its appointed course. I wished that I could find *my* right course. I didn't know that I was already in a learning process that would, in time, begin to open the understanding that I longed for. Years later, I learned that the problem was not that anyone was holding me back: it was that I had so much to learn before I could even *begin* to address the questions that tormented me. And my questions were deeper than typical college professors of that era could address.

Shortly before the end of that academic year, as warm spring weather replaced the darkness of winter, I went walking alone in the woods. The sunlight poured through the trees overhead. The world was coming alive again. Standing in solitude below the trees, bathed again in golden light, I felt the experience of awakening returning as strongly as before. Joyfully, I walked barefoot on the earth. Every part of my body responded to the new life surging around me. My spirits soared. It was a very personal experience in which the nature spirits seemed to reach out and welcome me. When I returned to the campus, I had only one thought: to write the story of my experience, to seize it on paper before the subtle feelings slipped from memory. I knew that this experience was important, but that if "normal" people had such experiences, then they didn't talk about it. I wrote about that experience, expressing as best I could the wonder and gratitude that I felt.

A friend told me I should show what I'd written to Dr. Clifford Crump, a semi-retired astronomy professor and a Quaker. I was hesitant to share such personal thoughts with a professor whom I didn't know, but fearing to miss any guidance I might find, I did ask Dr. Crump to meet with me. I think he understood that I worried that I might be losing my grip on reality. He read my story while I sat with him in his office. Then to my astonishment he thanked me for sharing it with him. He said he didn't fully understand my experience, but, he explained, "It's clear to me that you are a *seeker*, which is something rare." I had to ask what he thought I was seeking, but he said he didn't know. He urged me to go on seeking even if it was difficult. He told me that some purpose was behind it, and I would surely learn more in time. I believed him. As a result, I could see myself as a seeker, rather than as someone losing his mind. When I left his office, Dr. Crump warmly wished me well and embraced me, an unusual gesture, I thought, for a professor. He was the only person at this college who was able to give me any insight at all into my quest.

My questions were not to be resolved for another two and a half years. My meeting with Dr. Crump was therefore of great importance to me, letting me believe that, if I went on seeking, then eventually I would find something worth the effort. I felt relieved of anxiety, and I felt newly empowered to give this seeking a priority in my life. This was a major change from the conventional endeavors of young adults: to allow my own unusual interests to guide my life choices. I did this cautiously and thoughtfully, but I no longer had any fear or hesitation about leaving the beaten path of material success.

One understanding that came from this college year was that no intellectual formula, no philosopher's dissertation, was going to satisfy me. Only something actually experienced, like my experiences of nature, could teach me about reality, about who and what I was and what I needed. Even though this college was a rich learning environment, with progressive ideas in abundance and lots of opportunities for interaction with other students and with teachers, I never found my own ground there. However, there was a series of guest lecturers who brought interesting ideas with them, one of whom gave me the idea for my next phase of life.

To seek and to find is no sign of madness;
It is one of life's pleasures, one of life's treasures.
Relentlessly searching to understand mysteries—
    What makes us human?
    How to be conscious?
    The meaning of love?
    Is there truth to be found?
These are hard questions. Enigmas abound.

CHAPTER THREE

A Seeker in the Civil Rights Movement

1964–1965

At Earlham College I met Rev. James Bevel, a civil rights activist and colleague of Dr. Martin Luther King Jr. In his guest lecture Rev. Bevel spoke contemptuously of academic learning as a mere social courtesy, a capitulation to social norms: as he expressed it, "learning how to use a knife and fork." He told how the young black men and women in Georgia, Alabama, and Mississippi were standing up to fire hoses and police dogs to demand the respect of full citizenship and the abolition of Jim Crow laws, through which white supremacy was enforced by the state and local governments. He said that many whites from the North had joined them in support, and these young people were learning together the greatness of being human. I was galvanized by his blunt words. College was not meeting my personal needs, and I wanted to support this political movement and learn from these dynamic people. Perhaps there I might learn more about truth, love, and consciousness.

At the end of that academic year I left college, with no thought of returning. I left chemistry and philosophy behind. In September, 1964, I became a volunteer in the Student

Nonviolent Coordinating Committee, SNCC, an influential part of the Council of Federated Organizations, COFO, a civil rights organization active in Mississippi. That very spring, three civil rights workers had been brutally murdered in that state. I can only imagine the fear my parents must have felt when I told them of my decision, and yet they supported my plan. They even helped me with a little money for my living expenses.

The civil rights movement was in full swing across the American Deep South and other states. It was a daily feature in the national television news. Dr. Martin Luther King Jr. was still the national spokesman for the movement, and he was awarded the Nobel Peace Prize while I was in Mississippi. His civil rights work centered on the state of Georgia, and took place within another organization, the Southern Christian Leadership Conference. In Mississippi, where the movement was coordinated mostly by SNCC, we didn't have his charismatic leadership at the top. The movement in Mississippi was deliberately run in a bottom-up loose structure. The other workers were full of the energy and resolve that characterized the civil rights movement. Like me, they were nearly all young, unpaid volunteers. Many were white, but most were black. Nearly all the most influential leaders were black, which I thought was appropriate. These were serious people, who seemed to sense that their actions really could affect the future. Sometimes they placed their lives in jeopardy for this cause. This was to become the most intense year of education I had yet undertaken. In that electric environment, focused entirely on political and economic issues, I didn't speak of my interest in consciousness or my need to understand life deeply. The seeker became hidden, but was very much alive within.

I had the privilege of meeting some of the leaders in Mississippi. They were intelligent visionaries, social philosophers, and political activists. At a conference, I met one of these men. I found him sitting amid a small group of people who were wrapped in his words when I joined them. He was black and wore blue denim overalls to show his identity with common people, although, from his articulate way of speaking, I took him to be well educated. He spoke very softly. His poetic language painted pictures in my mind of the high value of every human life—even the poorest. He had an infectious vision, somewhat like that of Martin Luther King's "dream," of a strong and compassionate society based on human understanding and caring, which he shared with all who would listen. I met him only this once. I didn't learn his name. He was very unassuming, and it was only later that I realized I had met a truly revolutionary thinker. Within a few minutes I was able to see his beneficent vision for American society. I carried it away with me. I still carry it. (A bit of historical research leads me to believe that this visionary leader might have been Bob Moses.)

At another organizational meeting in Mississippi, I made a proposal that was promptly opposed by one of the leaders. I didn't take this personally, as I understood the give-and-take of group decision-making, and I was rather a newcomer anyway. I was surprised when, a few minutes later, the same leader walked over to me and said he hoped he hadn't offended me. Then he shared some personal thoughts about the issue in question. I don't remember the issue, but I do remember being warmed by his concern for my feelings, and so, by example, I learned a lesson about human sensitivity. A year or two later, that leader became an internationally known civil rights activist. His name was Stokely Carmichael.

ROLE PLAYING

I was assigned to a group working in Gulfport, Mississippi. In this urban part of the state, there was less danger of violent Ku Klux Klan activity than there was in more rural parts of Mississippi. I lived with a black family and joined the other workers nearly every day for lunch at the home of a minister, John Self, who was also one of the workers. There, we talked about many things, sometimes planning our projects, sometimes just getting to know one another. We were a mixed group and were aware of our racial and cultural differences. Sometimes, in spontaneous play, we would fall into role-playing. We used dialects and racial slurs in our role-playing. Each player could to some extent feel the emotions within a culture he or she was unfamiliar with.

I particularly remember one time when a black friend spoke to me in the voice of a white bigot—sneering at the black man's social inferiority. He clearly wished me to play the part of the black man, and I was willing. I felt his power over me, how, in any black-white conflict the white man was always right, the black man wrong. Such was my perception of the culture at that time and place. I answered in the meek voice of the subservient black man—in dialect, as nearly as I could. I addressed him as "sir." I felt fear, knowing my helplessness. I'm sorry to say it, but I actually felt myself to be inferior. How readily that role took over my sense of self! Still, at some level, I knew that I, the black man, had as much human worth as he, but I closely felt the role I played, feeling the injustice—indeed the unreality—of our social roles. Not only as a white man, but as a black man, I was playing a role. It was too dangerous not to play. If I had been more courageous, I might have taken the role of a strong black man who spoke back as a calm and equal human being, with words such as, "Well, my friend, we are both God's creatures. Let us treat each other with respect." I wonder how that "white bigot," in the body of a black man, would have responded.

Afterward, I wondered how black people might relate to me, as a white person. I felt I was not someone who needed to boost his ego by feeling superior to others, but still I had to ask, how much advantage did I have, and did I use it unfairly in any way? These were necessary questions in that culture. We civil rights workers were there to question and confront segregationist culture with our marches, our teaching, our voter registration efforts, our freedom songs, and our personal learning about human worth.

In role playing, such as I've described, I caught a glimpse of the face of the white power structure as seen through a black person's eyes, a face that was not sensitive to the human feelings of a black person. If, in role playing, I was criticized for being an oppressor, then it wasn't truly me who was being judged, but was only a role that might be projected onto me in another person's mind. That's in the nature of role playing. But then who or what was "me" as distinguished from the roles I played here, or even my roles in normal life? I couldn't answer that, and I would have felt more secure if I did know who and what I was. I think this racial divide will remain in America until we can talk about these things and learn to see each other more truly—that is to see each other's *inner* natures, to understand that other people are very much like ourselves and are worthy of respect, as I learned more deeply, years later, through my spiritual education.

THE FREEDOM SCHOOL

My first assignment in Mississippi was to start a "freedom school." When I was given this job I asked, "What should I teach?" I was told, "black history." I was so ignorant that I replied, "There *is* such a thing?" My reply must have made a very bad impression. I was given a text book with the curt advice, "Read it. Teach it." I walked to the local segregated black high school, and after school had let out I invited some students to come to a class on black history that I would hold weekly, after school, in the school library. A few students came. I was open about being ignorant of this subject myself, admitting that I, too, was a product of conventional education. I said we could learn together. Probably it was better that way. Sitting around a conference table, we enjoyed learning of the many contributions black people had made to science, industry, and politics, most of which were ignored in the normal school classes throughout the country. And, of course, we discussed the history of slavery and the culture of suppression, including Jim Crow laws, many still being enforced in Mississippi and other parts of the country. It was important for these students to understand the historical origin of their own second-class status in American society, so they could realize that there was nothing wrong with themselves personally or culturally.

In one of our classes I brought a white object and a black object and placed them on the table. I asked that we all put our arms out on the table and notice each other's skin colors, and note the colors of the two objects. Then I asked who here had truly black skin and who had white skin. By making this comparison we could readily see that none of us had skin that was truly either black or white. Then I gave a brief lecture about words, and how sometimes the meanings of words departed from the reality of our sense perceptions, having hidden judgmental meanings that we might not even notice but which still might unconsciously affect our values and self image. Racial designations often had such judgmental, hidden meanings. This teaching experience was challenging, but I found it to be something quite in my nature.

VOTER REGISTRATION

Another assignment I was given had me going alone for weeks, door-to-door in the black community, encouraging people to register to vote. At the time, Mississippi had instituted a form of voter suppression, a written literacy test that effectively barred the blacks from voting. It wasn't just the difficulty of the test itself, which used the formal language of the state constitution, but it was a reminder that if you were black, then your vote wasn't wanted. One's employer might also be notified of the attempt to register to vote. It took courage for a black person even to ask to register to vote in such a culture. For the few who were bold enough, I offered to tutor them individually, to help them read the test if needed and learn the answers to the questions. These were not the energetic young people in the civil rights movement, but older people who had lived with racial prejudice for decades and had adapted to it. A few people accepted my challenge and the tutoring. As I talked to them I asked myself, by what right could a young northern white man confront their generations of having to accommodate the unreality of racial role playing? As I worked with them I could sometimes see them struggling to grow inside. The battle hymn of the civil rights movement was "We Shall Overcome." This meant more than just overcoming Jim Crow laws. I watched these older people struggle within to *overcome* a social orientation that had placed them in the position of supposedly inferior people. I saw them take upon themselves the responsibilities of a voting citizen. Sometimes I told them how much I admired what they were doing. It was the hidden seeker within me, I think, that understood the individual human struggles that I saw.

Once, while I was experiencing this understanding, an inner voice, like another mind within my own mind, spoke to me in thought and said, "David, you, too, must overcome." The presence of this voice didn't bother me, but its demand did. Immediately, I argued with it in thought, "But I've already registered to vote." The voice let me know that there was more that I must do if I, too, wished to become a free man. Just *what* I must do remained a puzzle, but the seeker within me didn't forget what I had been told. This happened while I was sitting with a man I was tutoring in his home. As we spoke together, there was little time for thinking, but somehow that current of thought played out in my mind. There was something real in these thoughts. It was not just my mind spinning imaginations, but something deeper, truer, and I felt it. That was one of the early experiences that drove me in an urgent search for an understanding of what lay behind the superficiality of the everyday world. I really did want to know what the voice had meant—what more there was that I must do to overcome. And I didn't yet feel that I was a free man. *And, what was this inner voice?*

As far as I know, only two of the people I tutored actually went downtown to face the voting registrar; both passed the test. I felt proud of them for their courage and accomplishment, and yet it was a frustrating time for me because our stated goal was to help create a voting base that could make a difference in future elections. Two new voters would hardly turn the tide. Fortunately, a few months after I left Mississippi, the federal Voting Rights Act of 1965 was enacted by Congress, outlawing literacy tests. I heard then that people got registered to vote by the busload. I like to think that I, and other civil rights workers like me, had helped awaken an interest in voting.

A reader might wonder why I speak only of "black" people, not "African-Americans." I once raised this very question of language with one of my acquaintances in the black community where I lived and worked. She had no difficulty answering that question. She told me, "I'm *not* African. I'm American. And I want to be respected *as* an American." Her words made so much sense that for me the question was definitively closed, and now I seldom use the word "African-American." It is also true, as I pointed out to my black history students, that "black" people are very rarely black, nor do they have the negative attributes that we associate with "blackness." Racial identity is mostly cultural: there is very little biological difference.

My civil rights work also took me briefly to Washington,

DC, where, on Capitol Hill, as a silent partner in some legislative advocacy, I observed those with better skills than I had, speaking to members of Congress about proposed laws. I saw that in this setting the use of restrained, soft speech, careful reasoning, and dignity was more persuasive than aggressive confrontation. I photographed this activity and reported back to the community where I worked in Mississippi about how the legal work was done, how it affected them, and how their votes strengthened themselves and their advocates. I could not have learned more about political science in an entire semester of college study.

As I became acquainted with my fellow civil rights workers I came to see them from the inside—I saw the inner person, the person we usually hide from others—and I saw that each was tender within, vulnerable, loving, wise. I noticed that this inner self was a more permanent, more stable feature of personality than was our shifting social roles. I think it was the danger we shared, of arrest, even of being killed, that brought out this honesty between us. Soldiers in wars often come to see each other that way, I think, for the same reasons. Each person had this inner self, and it was very similar from one person to another, across racial and even gender lines. I wondered, what was this inner self, and how did it affect our lives? I asked myself whether this inner self was something real, or whether my imagination was being carried away. I had no more idea about that inner aspect of others than I had about my own true nature. I couldn't discuss these interests with my fellow workers, who seemed to be focused entirely on social and political changes in the world. Only the seeker wondered to himself.

I sometimes discussed my experiences and thoughts with the lady whose family I lived with in Mississippi, Lilly Belle Flowers. Once our conversation turned to religion. She asked me, "Do you love Jesus?"

I didn't think of myself as religious at all, much less as a Christian. I answered, "No."

She replied, "Yes you do."

I think a surprised look was my only response.

With a smile she continued, "I can tell."

I respected Lilly Belle, so I couldn't dismiss what she had said. Perhaps she had spotted *my* inner person, the seeker, whom I had tried to keep hidden.

ARRESTED

While in Mississippi I participated in a freedom march in the state capital, Jackson. After a series of marches in which the local residents and civil rights workers had been arrested and sometimes beaten in jail so that few would march again, a call went out to the civil rights workers all over the state asking us to continue the marches. Meanwhile, our lawyers were trying to get a federal court injunction against the city of Jackson to stop these arrests. But because all the protesters had been bailed out and would not march again, the federal court now felt no urgency to act. We were told that, if we volunteered for this action, we would almost certainly be arrested and possibly beaten. Still, many of the workers answered the call. In many parts of Mississippi arrest was a routine hazard of civil rights work. I hadn't been arrested yet. I felt that this was my test.

Two days later I was in Jackson, getting into position for the march. Those around me seemed calm and brave. But my stomach was a knot of fear. I wondered if I could live with myself if I just slipped away. I thought of my coworkers in Gulfport, of my parents who were encouraging me, and of my Uncle Henry who had spent a long time in prison for his protests. I decided that in spite of fear and danger, I must march.

We started walking together in a nearly empty street, carrying signs saying "Freedom Now," "End Segregation," etc., and singing freedom songs. There was nothing inflammatory in our statements. Within a few blocks we were stopped by a police barricade and placed under arrest. After a long wait, four or five trucks drove up, large flatbed trucks that had large, inexpertly welded cages built on them with locking doors in the backs. They looked rather new and had evidently been built as a response to the civil rights movement. This fleet of trucks spoke for the racist power structure: *We are prepared to arrest thousands of you.* The demonstrators were made to get into the cages, and the trucks drove off, with several motorcycle policemen following each, apparently to make sure that none of us escaped. They seemed unaware that we actually intended to be arrested and had no interest in escaping.

As we rode through the city we sang freedom songs to keep up our courage. Thousands of bystanders, black and white, saw us pass. Once, when no one else was present, we sang directly to the motorcycle policemen following us:

> O Johnson, you know you can't jail us all!
> O Johnson, segregation's bound to fall!
>
> *(Johnson: The song addresses Governor Paul B. Johnson of Mississippi, to us a personification of Jim Crow culture, not President Lyndon B. Johnson.)*

We were taken to the city's agricultural fairgrounds, which had two huge exhibit buildings that had been strongly screened to serve as mass prison camps. Perhaps they wanted us to see that they intended to *try* to "jail us all." We spent three days there, men in one building, women in the other. The women, in one loud voice, sang freedom songs from their building. We men could hear them, and we sang back with another verse of the same song. I felt an exhilaration of unity in our singing.

Our lawyers talked to us individually and offered to bail us out if we asked for that, but reminded us that our being under arrest was needed to get the federal court injunction we sought, and it was a part of our protest statement. They explained that the federal court probably wouldn't act against the City of Jackson if no one were under arrest, and that each person who stayed encouraged everyone else. Very few chose to leave.

At night we were given thin mattresses over the concrete floor to sleep on, but in the morning we were ordered to stack them. This left us nothing but the concrete floor to sit on, so on the next morning, against orders, we sat on our mattresses. The guards roughly dragged them from under us. Apparently, they decided that one of us was the leader of this disobedience and that he should be separated from us. The man they had singled out was called to the door. When he realized their intention, he made an excuse to return to the rest of us for a moment. We thought that if he were taken away he might be beaten, and we should try to prevent it. So he sat on the floor with his back to a wall, and the rest of us, more than fifty young men, black and white, made a pile of bodies over and around him with linked arms and legs. We waited, and the guards called for reinforcements.

At last they approached us with nightsticks in hand. One by one they removed each of us from the pile by holding our necks between their nightsticks and their bodies. Then, pulling backwards, they dragged us from the pile. It was painful, and some of us were bleeding afterwards. Our pile gave way slowly. I was surprised when my turn came, because I was dragged by the arm rather than the neck and not with a nightstick. If I had been black, I think I would have been treated more harshly. Or, perhaps, there was some divine intervention. I could feel the policeman's hands trembling as he pulled me. I think that for a moment, as we touched, I received his thoughts—that to some extent he understood the rightness of our actions. I felt sorry that he had to do the job he was doing. I didn't fight or struggle as some of us did. In the end they got the man they were after, but they got our strong statement of unity also.

Perhaps the police thought that we would be more subdued without our leader, but with our experience in bottom-up organizing, we didn't feel powerless when our leader was removed. We still felt at-one with our group, able to act decisively together. Bottom-up organizing has its advantages, but top-down organizing, when there is a strong, wise leader, has advantages too. I think that the two systems might work well together, but that is rarely attempted.

The next day, the City of Jackson received a federal court injunction to stop the arrests of civil rights marchers. This injunction was our victory. It was for this that we had exposed ourselves to arrest and had refused bail. We were released the same day. Many of the citizens of Jackson resumed their own marches, no longer fearing arrest. I never learned what happened to the leader who was taken away. To the best of my knowledge, we were never formally charged with any crime.

I'm grateful to have had this brief exposure to a strong political movement, and further, for my experience of black culture, which isn't easy to understand for a white person living mainly in white society.

RACIAL PREJUDICE

I haven't yet spoken of the hurts, both physical and emotional, that racism inflicts on black culture, but I surely felt those hurts as they were experienced by my fellow workers as if they had happened to me. As I write this chapter, a half-century later, I feel again the anger, the wrongness, the shame, and the sadness that I felt then, seeing the effects of racial prejudice up close. Old age has kindly brought to me a sense of detachment from most of the negative experiences in my life, but the feelings of hurt that I shared in the black community are still raw in my memory. Anger won't cure this cancer on American culture, although anger is present. Love, justice, and time might cure it. After ten months of work in the civil rights movement, I could no longer bear all the repetitive hurts that my coworkers suffered daily or weekly. As a white person, I was able to shelter myself from those hurts by returning home, and I did so, although most of my black coworkers had no such escape.

I have been told, quite seriously, that racial prejudice is now a thing of the past. But to my eyes prejudice remains deeply embedded in parts of American culture, currently re-emerging as the white supremacy movement, spreading the old fears and hatreds, finding sympathy in the fears of many people, and even finding places of power in our government. Until human sympathy becomes much stronger in American culture, racial prejudice will remain. Prejudice will be transcended only when we, as a multiracial culture, learn to see other people as conscious entities—as spiritual beings like ourselves, worthy of respect. I see no other cure. I still have hope that such spiritual growth is possible in our culture, but it's a slow process.

It's been brought to my attention that racial prejudice is only one aspect of a much wider social sickness of inadequate human empathy and respect. I expect that this is true. Racial prejudice is the aspect of this social sickness that I have been most personally exposed to. The remedy of cultural spiritual growth, such as I have applied in my own life, should address many forms of injustice as people begin to respect each other more. Spiritual growth is the main subject of this memoir. It's something that begins with individuals but can readily spread through social contacts to the wider culture, if people choose to embrace it. Mississippi has a bad reputation for racial discrimination, but not all the white people there were bigots. I was once stopped by a white policeman, not to arrest me, but to give me some valid advice on living safely as a civil rights activist in that state. I also had a brief association with a white church group that took a positive interest in the movement. I believe that there were probably many white people in that state who rejected Jim Crow culture, but to speak up forcefully could have brought down public censure, ostracism, or worse.

My experiences in Mississippi increased my perception of human worth and better focused my still unanswered questions of truth, love, and consciousness. Moreover, they gave me an opportunity to put into practice what I had learned only as theory from the Quakers: nonviolent direct action and occasionally civil disobedience. Following the civil rights movement, most Jim Crow laws were done away with. White-only drinking fountains became a thing of the past: drinking fountains were removed altogether—along with lunch counters. Even so, many discriminatory practices remain, such as as voter suppression laws presented as voter security, subtle and blatant discrimination in banking and housing, a cultural deficit in education, and police profiling. Still, the civil rights movement was one step toward the creation of a compassionate society. I've come to see that movement as one of America's greatest successes. I'm thankful to have had a small part in it. I left Mississippi in June 1965.

Can there be peace without human respect?
Strife must be present while injustice is flaunted.
The civil rights movement exposed the sickness
That had been in the dark for hundreds of years.
Change would not come without clear demonstration
Of who was hurt and why it was happening,
Brought to the conscience of a whole nation.

CHAPTER FOUR

Intellectual Struggle

1966–1968

In Mississippi, I learned rapidly about human nature, society, and politics, and I learned it without the aid of schools or teachers. I wanted to return to college, but I wondered whether any college existed where I could use my newly found independent learning abilities and where I could pursue my specific interests. My basic questions of truth, love, and consciousness were still unanswered, and they rankled in my mind. And the newer questions of social justice and of the inner nature of human beings that the civil rights movement had brought to my attention still challenged me to address them. Was it even possible that an academic setting could cast light on these questions? A friend suggested Goddard College in Vermont, a very unusual college for determined, independent thinkers. I visited there and felt that in such a fiercely independent setting there was room for me to grow. I spent two years there, beginning in the spring of 1966. At Goddard, I found students ferreting out new, under-explored crannies of knowledge, or finding and developing new, more inclusive paradigms. I, too, was looking for a new paradigm, a new way of understanding life.

Some fellow students suggested that whatever else I did,

I should be sure to take a course called "General Semantics." I signed up for it in my first semester. This course was concerned with levels of abstraction: a picture of an object is more abstract than the object itself; the word for an object is not the object either. That seems obvious until we examine how often we take the word as the very object itself in our thoughts. A central idea in this course was that our use of words, mentally or socially, affects our perceptions and sometimes even overrides our sense experiences, much as I had explained in my "freedom school" in Mississippi, using the black and white objects. In order to overcome these tendencies, the professor emphasized perceiving in the here-and-now. We had exercises in awareness of perceptions and awareness of our own thought processes. One such exercise was as simple as chewing a cracker without swallowing for some minutes. We were to write about what we tasted, what we felt in its texture, what we had thought: in general, what we had experienced. This focus on learning directly from experience reinforced the learning skills I had developed in Mississippi, and helped prepare me for my next major lesson, which, however, was still a few months ahead.

In another General Semantics class session, a teaching assistant introduced a series of optional seminars that would run parallel to the larger class, and he invited class members to take part. The assignment for the first meeting would be for each participant to write down and then speak about all his or her personal secrets to the group. He said there should be plenty of material produced by this assignment, and others to come, for intensive examination of misperceptions brought about through word use—or misuse. I felt that this kind of optional challenge would bring out the serious students, and interesting things were likely to happen. I wondered whether I was up to speaking about my secrets, but I thought that if I were going to benefit from this course I had better dive into it. I signed up for those seminars, as did four or five other students. At the first meeting, one after another, we spoke of our secrets. The group was full of tension. But then one student produced a small bag of candy and passed it around. We all laughed out loud, recognizing his intention to facilitate a more relaxed mood through sharing something pleasant. A few minutes later, this group developed a trusting, accepting relationship.

The most difficult secrets for me to talk about were my inner feelings. Most other students spoke of things they had done that they kept secret, but my secrets had mostly to do with my love and respect for other people, while still fearing their censure. I was still fearful of exposing my own inner being, and I thought that if I expressed myself too openly I might end up being hurt. But I also thought that to do so would help the purpose of this seminar, and I must try it and see where it led. At worst, I thought, I could always drop out of the seminar. But to my surprise, the others were appreciative of what I said. They felt I had opened a new avenue for our investigation, and one student, who had already spoken and could have remained quiet, responded by speaking of some of his own secret feelings, which he hadn't previously thought to do. In years following this class, such group exercises became rather popular in therapeutic and even religious settings. This seminar led me to become more aware of the insides of people, our secret thoughts, emotions, and longings—and, as I had sensed before in Mississippi, how much people's inner natures are very much alike. Accidentally, as it seemed, I was stepping back into the questions of people's inner sides: I had seen, in my fellow civil rights workers, their inner sides, their vulnerable emotional sides, the aspect of each person that tends to be hidden away, sometimes even from themselves. I had asked myself why each person's inner side seemed so much alike, so universal, and I had wondered what part these inner sides played in our lives. Now, I found I was in no better position to answer those questions, but more than ever I felt they were important, and I put them on a front burner for more careful consideration.

I also attended weekly seminars in expressive dance and spent one whole weekend with several other students deliberately and sensitively exploring each other's and our own emotions. Fellow students organized these activities, which were deeply engaging to me.

PSYCHOLOGY

I began to focus on the subject of psychology, thinking that if I could fully understand the inner self, then I might be well on the way to becoming a clinical psychologist, which would be both a source of income and a way of being of service to others. I realized, of course, that the inner self was not something physical: something that could be identified and located in the body. I became a senior teaching assistant for a psychology seminar class. The professor just wanted me to ask difficult questions, a role that I relished. In those days psychologists were anxious to be recognized as scientists, and that meant adopting a materialistic view of life: that only things that were physical, or had roots in the physical, were real. This view constituted the basis of the behaviorist school of psychology, which, according to the Merriam-Webster dictionary, "takes the objective evidence of behavior (such as measured responses to stimuli) as the only concern of its research and the only basis of its theory without reference to conscious experience."[3] This approach dominates psychology even today.

In focusing on the physical body and the objective side of behavior, psychologists had somehow to account for the mind or consciousness (which are treated as the same phenomenon by most psychologists), so consciousness was taken to be something that emerged naturally from the complexity of the physical brain. I've read about complexity theory and the study of chaotic interactions. While the occasional "emergence" of orderly phenomena within very complex systems is well established for chaos theory, I have never been comfortable with this "emergent" concept of consciousness arising from purely physical, nonconscious processes. Of course, in chapter 2, I did speak of "conscious water," and I was serious, but I have never thought of physical matter as having consciousness comparable to that of a higher life-form. I doubt if the nature of consciousness can ever be properly understood from the interactions of physical matter only. I thought that the most real part of a human was not the body or what the body did, but the *inner* person, where emotional or mental processing took place in the little understood but most important realm of consciousness. The psychology literature left me with a feeling of unreality: that the most central, most important question of psychology was left unaddressed. Then, I questioned whether I could embrace a school of thought that had what seemed to be such a gaping hole in its most basic tenants. Eventually, I turned away from psychology, as I had turned away from other academic disciplines.

In the sixties, of course, many people were experimenting with mind-altering drugs. A friend offered me marijuana, and it seemed like a good thing to try. After we had smoked for a while, he played a Beatles record. The music had a depth that I had never heard before. While I was still high, I went for a walk in the woods. It was autumn in Vermont, and that means color, but then, the brilliant colors I could see were overwhelming. The marijuana high reminded me of my experiences of awakening consciousness in nature, but to me it had a soporific effect, a *lessening* of consciousness, and it lacked the clarity and depth I had felt before.

I smoked marijuana several more times. Once, when I was having trouble completing some coursework, I began to feel anxious and guilty about my lack of work. I thought that

I'd feel better if I smoked some pot. I did smoke, and I felt fine. But then, while I was still high, a thought came to me: "Hey! I smoked that pot just as an escape. I really need to study, but now I have less concentration. What am I doing to myself?" That was the last time I smoked pot.

SHOULD I TAKE LSD?

I had heard that some people had mystical experiences when they took LSD. It seemed that using this drug might be a way to pursue my cherished dream of exploring consciousness and the inner self. I heard of some users who fell into mental illness, but I thought the exploration of consciousness was so important that it was worth some risk. There might be much to gain and much to lose. So I asked the question, *should I take LSD*? But, like so many of my urgent questions, I couldn't answer it then.

In pursuit of this question, I made use of the liberality of Goddard College: I designed a formal independent study about LSD, which would be one of my regular courses. I would study the productive experiences, and the frightening experiences, and the users who ended up in mental hospitals. I would write a research paper summarizing my findings, and perhaps I would find an answer to my question. But—surprise!—it was not easy to find a faculty adviser willing to supervise such a study. After several refusals, someone suggested that I ask Dave York, a biology instructor. At his office I found his wife, Phyllis, who asked what I wanted to study. She had an engaging manner, and I soon found she had a bold, probing attitude. She seemed ready to listen and to speak for the professor.

I described my independent study plan to her, emphasizing that I wouldn't use the drug during the study, and I handed her my written proposal. She set it aside. With a level gaze, she asked about my *personal* reasons for wanting to study LSD. Wondering if it would get me thrown out on my ear, I told her of the decision I was trying to make. Then she said, "Dave will do this with you." I was surprised that without asking him she would commit her husband to an endeavor that could risk his professional reputation. As I got to know them better, I saw that they worked together in a remarkable partnership of two strong people.

So Dave became my study advisor, but Phyllis took just as much interest in my progress. During the next several months I learned all I could about the various effects of the drug. My sources ranged from Timothy Leary's writings to medical literature. I thought that a clear-cut answer should emerge as to the value versus the risk of LSD. The opinions I read were very polarized, and many different factors seemed to affect the frightening reactions that some people had, making it very hard to evaluate what effect the drug might have on me. In those days it was just becoming known that LSD actually damages (or at least changes) the brain. It was *not* yet well known that it might take years for the brain to fully recover, if the drug were frequently used. If that had been clear to me then, I might not have considered using LSD at all.

While I was studying LSD, I went one evening to visit a fellow student, a friend. He had led the weekend seminar I mentioned earlier that explored emotions, and I had much respect for him. He was also studying psychology, as I was at the time. He and I had discussed whether or not to take LSD; it was a question he was asking too. I found him in his room. He told me he had made up his mind and had taken LSD a few minutes before. I felt terribly drawn to share this experience with him, but he told me he wanted to be alone. So I arranged to meet with him the next morning and left.

Over breakfast, he told me he had been awake all night

with the drug experience. I could see he was still wrapped in the ethereal mood of it. He did his best to describe the experience, which seemed to be a typical psychedelic experience. Then he said, "Last night, I saw the door to insanity open, like a physical doorway. I was very curious, and I almost walked through. If I had, I don't think I would have been able to return to a regular social role very soon. Even now, I feel drawn back to it." At the end of our talk he said, "I see now why people say this is a dangerous drug. You should think twice before using it." Even though "thinking twice," or even more, was the purpose of my study, I felt sobered by his words, but thinking of the understanding the drug might give me, I felt drawn to the experience even more than before. In fact, the urgency of making the choice became an agony for me.

What I was learning didn't answer my quandary—it deepened it. Dave and Phyllis invited me to their home and just listened as I poured out how torn I felt. They offered no advice as to what conclusion I should draw, leaving the responsibility with me. To this day I'm grateful that I was left free to struggle with this question, because, in the end, I learned exactly what I needed from this study, and it was not something that academicians would normally think of.

My friend who took LSD suggested that I talk with another faculty member, Dr. Ken Schramm. I sought him out. After I told him the question I was struggling with he replied, "It depends on what you consider *sacred*." He was using that word as an anthropologist might, but I thought of myself as a nonreligious person, so my first reaction was the thought, "What does the word 'sacred' have to do with me?" But that persistent inner voice, not speaking words this time, merely nudged me with its elbow in thought, suggesting that I should explore the meaning of that word. That opened a new phase in my search, one that eventually helped me to a conclusion.

THE ASHRAM

I had some friends at the college who met weekly to practice a kind of meditation. I attended one or two of their meetings and learned something of their method of focusing attention at various places in the body and listening to the messages the body gives. I enjoyed the company of these students, although this method of meditation was of only moderate interest to me. One evening, this group went to visit an ashram, a spiritual center near the college, and they asked me to come. I had never before heard of this place. Apparently this was a curiosity side trip for most of them, but it became a revelation to me. Driving at night through unlit, forested roads, we finally entered an old farmhouse, decorated with natural objects, where a nice lady told us about spiritual meditation. She described a form of meditation in which one could actually see Light within, Light from a higher, more spiritual plane than the physical. This was a meditation that could give insights into the real nature of human beings, of one's own self. That was the very crux of my many questions!

At this ashram, more than anything else, I was attracted by a presence—a golden light in the room, probably not anything physical. I had often seen this light before during my years of seeking. I had learned that when I saw this light that something special was close, and I should stop and let it emerge. Then a message from within came to me that in this unusual place there was something important for me to learn. I knew I would have to return alone and learn more.

A week later, I went back to the ashram. I met the same lady, who later became my friend, but who asked to remain anonymous in these pages. She told me, "The kind of meditation your group is practicing will take you further into body consciousness. But in spirituality our goal is to rise *above* the body." I replied, "This is our meeting night, but I came here." This teaching began to answer many of the questions with which I was struggling at the time, and most of the remainder of this memoir concerns my exploration of spirituality. So I'll go into a little detail here about those teachings.

She explained that this ashram was dedicated to Sant Kirpal Singh (1894-1974), who was himself spiritually accomplished and was a living Master spiritual teacher of meditation, able to help and guide the spiritual student into higher states of consciousness. He lived in Delhi, India. He presented spirituality as an experiential study without rites and rituals, a teaching that could serve people of any religion, or even people like myself, of no specific religion. This is an ancient teaching from India referred to as *Sant Mat* (pronounced "sunt mut" in India, meaning teaching of the saints). Sant Kirpal Singh grew up in the Sikh religion, and he used many of the concepts put forth by Guru Nanak, the first of the line of ten Sikh gurus. But Sant Kirpal Singh didn't try to convert people to Sikhism. In fact he seemed to be equally comfortable quoting Christian, Muslim, or Buddhist esoteric scriptures, and he spoke with the confidence of someone who had experienced for himself the reality behind those teachings. Curiously, I looked at photos of Master Kirpal. He had a full beard, wore the traditional turban of the Sikhs, and had a kind and intelligent face and an upright bearing. At that time, he was 73 years old.

My friend played tape recordings of Master Kirpal's discourses in English and read aloud from his books and circulars. He said that we are not our bodies, and in meditation we can gradually learn to separate ourselves from our bodies and experience our own nature, which is spiritual. My friend gave me some elementary meditation instructions, as taught by Sant Kirpal Singh, and I meditated briefly. I experienced myself as a conscious being, living in a body, but as distinct from the body. I found it very interesting and peaceful. She told me that to follow this spiritual path one must adopt a vegetarian diet, since, like us, animals are conscious, and consciousness is an aspect of the divine. During the next week I cautiously tried eliminating meat and eggs from my diet. I liked the idea of not killing animals, and I felt I was still getting the nutrients I needed. With only a little effort, I became a strict vegetarian: no meat, fish, fowl, or eggs, but dairy products were permitted, as no taking of life was involved. Increasingly, I was turning toward the Sant Mat teachings as a way to address the many questions with which I struggled.

THE PREDICAMENT OF HUMANKIND

I learned that Sant Mat had its own creation story, with its own version of how human beings came to be reduced from originally fully conscious, blissful beings to a semiconscious, or nearly unconscious and deeply troubled state. Nearly every religion has explanations for the world and for the state of humankind. Here was another account, presented in such a way that didn't deny other religious versions so much as it suggested that each version might have some truth, if only in an allegorical sense. I found this viewpoint respectable and attractive. I learned this explanation in bits and pieces, but I'll give a brief summary of it as I came to understand it:

In the beginning of creation there existed consciousness, a loving, blissful, divine consciousness and nothing but this consciousness, which is the foundation of creation. This consciousness was—is—what we have come to understand as God. This consciousness longed for relationship such as that found in union or in separation with other entities. So this consciousness expressed itself as many conscious entities, all "parts" of itself and not really separate, but having the illusion of separateness. These entities had all the attributes of the divine. They were "micro-gods," as Sant Kirpal Singh expressed it. These parts of God are what we have come to know as souls, the basis of life and consciousness in all living things, including humans. This divine consciousness then manifested from itself a wondrous creation consisting of planes of varying proportions of matter and consciousness, in which these seemingly separate souls could visit and have adventures: *learning* adventures, through which the souls could explore their own natures and ultimately recognize the Creator from which they emerged. The souls were given coverings—bodies—consisting of matter and mind that enabled them to interact with the substance of each of the planes where they visited or dwelt. For example, the *mind*-covering endowed those souls with intellect, judgment, and with qualities that encouraged them to focus attention on the substance of planes in which they found themselves, such as physical matter in the case of human beings. These coverings of the souls were not so much enhancements to perception as they were limitations on perception—filters to perception. Those souls that became humans were confined, in part, by their fates—the events of life that were inevitable. Still, humans were not puppets on controlling strings, but had a measure of free will, especially in the field of moral choices. God knew that the suffering the souls experienced in the illusion of their long separation from their source, while dwelling in various bodies, would ultimately lead them to yearn to seek out and reunite with their creator and recapture their original blissful state. However, the souls became familiar with their new environments and came to identify with their bodies and their surroundings, which, in error, they mistook as the sole reality of existence. That is the unhappy situation in which we humans—embodied souls, parts of God's own being, living in illusion—find ourselves today. And some of us are finding that desire to reunite with our blissful, divine source, while still living a full, responsible social life.

I, as a beginning student of this teaching and with no orientation in religion, had no immediate way either to confirm or disprove any such explanation of the world or the state of humankind. Still, I did find the Sant Mat version of creation and loss of consciousness to be interesting and attractive. I did give it some tentative credence. But when I did that, I also had to recognize that I was doing something similar to what many religious adherents did in what I contemptuously had called "blind faith." I had to recognize that I, too, had a need for some intellectual framework, even a tentative or experimental framework, within which I could make my exploration of spirituality—of consciousness. From that realization I gained a modicum of intellectual humility.

Sant Mat also embraced the idea of the Law of Karma, said to be a natural law of the universe: the idea that every thought, word, and deed affects the future of each soul. Its purpose is to make each embodied soul feel the effect of every thought, word, and deed performed and to bear the consequences of those actions in the same lifetimes or in future lifetimes, where those consequences might be burdensome ("bad karma") or welcome ("good karma") as perceived by the mind-ridden soul. For example, a person who murdered another in one lifetime might be required to be murdered himself in another lifetime. Or, someone who was very helpful to others might find generous helping hands in his future lives. There is an eye-for-an-eye kind of justice in this. The karmas then become part of the soul's experiences in one life or another, forming its fate for that lifetime. Those karmic fates must be lived through. As Sant Kirpal Singh explained, "Once the tracks are laid, the train must run on them." If the fate karmas were somehow removed, then the person's life would be over. In a lifetime, more karmas are typically created than can be resolved. The unresolved karmas accumulate in vast storage accounts from which they can be resolved in future lives, even while new karmas are being created. The teachers of Sant Mat say that through countless lifetimes the souls become imprisoned by these mounting credits and debits, which they must justly pay or receive.

However, the Law of Karma contains an escape clause: if embodied souls learn that it is actually not they but rather the Power overhead, God, that is the doer of their actions—that in reality there is no "I" within them but only divine consciousness—then no individual remains to bear the karmic consequences, and the karmic bonds simply fall away. Mere intellectual learning, mere blind faith, will not be sufficient to effect this realization: the lesson must be a concrete reality, coming from personal experience at the level of the soul. But how many souls can make such a profound realization on their own? Teachers are required: teachers who have pursued such a spiritual quest themselves and have mastered the meditation technique. Simpler things also help, they say: we can have thoughts and actions performed with no purpose of personal gain or pleasure. These don't involve karma. An intent that any reward should be laid at the feet of God also avoids karma, and meditation helps reduce the load. The spiritual Masters explain these things in detail and also directly help manage the aspirant's karmic account. If lived with care, the aspirant's life can end with no karma and no need to return in a future life to the physical plane, to resolve the karmic account.

The subject of spirituality answered many questions that my years of seeking had raised. In particular, as I practiced meditation, I found that again I was learning something about the inner person—in this case my own inner person. I began to feel the need to go deeply into this subject of inner consciousness and to learn this meditation technique. Further, this teaching gave me a way of understanding the word *sacred*, which I had been challenged to explore.

WHAT IS SACRED?

With the college semester drawing to a close, I felt I must reach some conclusion in my study of LSD. So, with my new understanding of spirituality, I focused intensely on the question of what was sacred to me. Why did I think that question was the key? I have never known for sure, but perhaps it was the inner "nudge" I received when the question was introduced. What was the source of that nudge, I didn't know, but I was beginning to take such inner messages seriously. I thought over the years of seeking: my experiences of consciousness in nature, my meeting with Dr. Crump, my experiences at Goddard College, in Mississippi, and at the ashram. For the first time, all these experiences fit together. I felt I had been led through a series of learning experiences that had brought me to a new understanding, and I realized then that I had been led from within, while the necessary worldly circumstances in which I could learn had also been provided. There was something within me that was seeking a new kind of knowledge—there was something that was me, yet was more than me—and its purpose, I thought, was the most important thing in my life. I was coming to *identify* with this inner self that was deeper than any previous knowledge of myself, and I now felt that *this* was something sacred. So the word 'sacred,' which I had so resisted, *did* have something to do with me after all. I wanted to let it work as it had been working during the years of my search, not to force my inner self open with drugs, but to trust it to help me grow into a more conscious person. This would perhaps be a slower approach to understanding, but that understanding would be earned from hard work and would be deeper, more real, more secure than an easily gained experience from a drug. Seeing that such an approach was possible and that a guide was available in the person of Sant Kirpal Singh, I no longer had any wish to take LSD. I had found a very interesting answer to my question about that drug, which was that there seemed to be, for me at least, a better way to explore consciousness.

I related my conclusions to Dave and Phyllis. At their

home we had a long talk about the thought process I had gone through. Phyllis asked many questions to learn how I arrived at my conclusion and probably to encourage further thought. I felt that she, especially, shared my excitement of discovery. Dave suggested that rather than writing a research paper, I might formally close my study by writing a paper on how I had made my decision. I wrote that paper and felt that for the first time in my life I was writing something that was of value to myself and possibly to others.

During this process of decision-making, I also had a dawning awareness that there was more than the rational mental process at work. In discovering something of the nature of that inner Power, I had empowered my own soul to some extent, which quickly grasped the reality of the spiritual learning process and the nature of psychedelic drugs. At the level of soul, the decision about LSD was made almost in an instant, but the *mental* processing—the finding of rational reasoning that would faithfully reflect the soul's process—took several days of hard thinking before I could write my paper. I now see that when my mind came to understand and appreciate what the soul valued, then mind and soul began to work together. The soul held much wisdom, and the mind could find ways to express it. It was exhilarating to experience soul and mind working together, although at the time I could not have expressed that integrative process in words. It was working at a level I didn't comprehend—but it was working!

What most excited me was the discovery that all my pressing questions were interrelated, and I was beginning to find tentative answers. My several questions about the inner self, such as the nature of the inner self, why I felt I was being led from within, why the inner self seemed to be so much alike between individuals, and what was sacred, now resolved into a single hypothetical concept: *There is a divine Power, an intelligent consciousness, intimately connected to each individual (even when suppressed or denied), not separate from individuals, but somehow transcending individuals, which had the purpose of growing the consciousness of individuals toward experiencing their true natures—of experiencing the interconnected nature of human beings and of experiencing that Power itself.* For a time, I put aside everything else I had learned about spirituality. This concept alone was big enough for me to absorb. Some readers, for whom this concept might already be something obvious, may smile at my sense of discovery, but that's where I stood in my spiritual understanding. To more rigorously prove or disprove that concept, even just to my own satisfaction, would probably be the work of a lifetime.

During the next semesters, in an effort to understand reality, I continued to use independent studies to explore and test the reality of the spiritual teachings. I tried to reconcile this study of subtle things with my intellectual understanding of the world. It took nearly a year just to become comfortable with the spiritual teachings. The subject was too important to me to leave any part of it untested. I finally concluded that my hypothesis was fully acceptable—as a hypothesis, not yet proved, but intuitively making sense. I became satisfied, at an intellectual level, that our physical experiences, our emotions, our thoughts, and our deepest spiritual experiences *all* have roots in an underlying spiritual reality that is universal to all people, and that was why the inner selves of people seemed so much alike to me. I became deeply engaged in this intellectual work, although few other people could understand its importance to me. Even my senior study, another independent study in my last semester, was devoted entirely to spirituality as presented by many writers from the East and the West.

Looking back, it seems a wonder that I found so much academic freedom at Goddard College. My mentors couldn't have known *what* I might conclude about LSD, nor perhaps did they understand what drove me in pursuit of spiritual understanding. Still, they seemed to recognize that I was pursuing some of the deepest questions of existence. I felt they trusted me, and they invested deeply in my education with their time and their intellectual guidance, keeping me more or less within the bounds of rational thought, while still giving me room to explore in thought as I felt necessary.

This exploration of spirituality ended my eight-year search for a teacher who could point me in the direction of the realities of life. I felt that Dr. Crump's assurance that I *would* find something was now fulfilled. This search had been a difficult time for me, but looking back I see that I learned a great deal. With my experiences of seeing life in nature I learned that there was a wonderful, spiritual side to life, of which normally I was quite unaware and to which I had no access that I could control. I came to value the consciousness that opened the spiritual aspect of life, and I sought more of it. In college I learned that it was acceptable for me to be a seeker: to restlessly search for understanding and consciousness. I learned that most of the academic disciplines were not going to answer my most pressing questions. I learned that I didn't want to pursue consciousness through drug experiences. In the civil rights movement I learned that there is something of great value in the inner person that we fearfully tend to hide from each other and sometimes even from ourselves, and at the ashram I learned that this inner person is most truly who we are. It was not enough to be told these things, as I am writing them: I had to experience these lessons in my life. Now, I had found my central interest in life, and with that everything else began making sense. I felt ready to learn about spirituality and to engage with a spiritual teacher. I believe that if I had learned about spirituality earlier, I would have dismissed the idea of a spiritual teacher, doubting that what he had to offer was what I was seeking, and once I had formed that idea it would have hardened in my mind for a long time. I would have thrown away an incredible opportunity. But as it worked out, I became ready to accept that teacher, to commit myself to a lifetime of learning and to a struggle to become a human being worthy of eventually finding the full consciousness that I longed for. As is often said in the philosophies of India: "When the chela [aspirant] is ready, the guru [teacher] appears." Little did I know then what an immense task I was undertaking, and yet no other life-work would have been so deeply fulfilling.

This student, now elderly, is critical of academic studies, but he still takes pleasure in some continued learning in all his abandoned fields. I now was focused on something akin to the Vedic concept of *sat chit anand* (truth, consciousness, bliss) and I was approaching it in some form of what Christians call "mysticism." This has remained my central interest in life.

Chemistry, the language of the alchemist, was considered and abandoned.
Philosophy, the language of those who truly confess their ignorance: cast aside.
Psychology, that purports to speak of the soul and yet denies it: forgotten.
Religious studies, with cages laid open for unwary seekers: dismissed.
And numerous other academic blind alleys: studied; measured; found wanting.
The world of the spirit had been closed by belief that it was unreal, irrational.
But experience of the numinous spirit came to the student.
This he must explore!
The stone that the academics rejected became the cornerstone of his life.

PART 2

Years with Sant Kirpal Singh Ji

CHAPTER FIVE

Spiritual Initiation

1967–1972

My friend at the ashram told me that if I were resolved to grow spiritually, I would need to be initiated by the Master, Sant Kirpal Singh Ji. The Master asked for no money for his initiation—it was a gift of love.

My friend encouraged me to write a letter to the Master in Delhi. I had no specific question, but wrote anyway, just to make contact. The Master cordially wrote back, advising me to study the literature available at the ashram and to maintain the vegetarian diet. He said, "Please try to adapt yourself to this kind of serene living in the larger interests of your spiritual progress." Gratefully, I felt that even though I had not yet even applied for initiation, he was already speaking to me as an accepted student.

The Master presented spirituality as a practice rather than as a religion. It's a specific meditative technique, with ethical disciplines, rather than merely a set of beliefs. And rituals were not a part of it. He didn't ask for blind faith in his teachings, but for enough of what might be called "experimental faith" that the aspirant would be willing to set up the required conditions in his life and to see what inner results could be achieved by that. He had written, "To believe in a thing or fact without troubling to investigate it does not in any way do credit to an intelligent man. . . . Any belief not based on personal experience and verification of the facts has little value."[4] This way of thinking, which promotes the value of personal experience, gave me confidence in this teacher.

Great thinkers have debated whether it is better to learn at the feet of an enlightened teacher or to remain an independent seeker, exploring within one's own guidance. I respect both these paths, as well as mixtures of the two. I believe we do have a responsibility to help ourselves as best we can, but I felt a need for guidance and companionship in my search. My years of seeking, without perceivable progress in growth of consciousness, had convinced me of my helplessness in this respect. In the spiritual tradition that I had found, there is much emphasis on the need for the help of a spiritual teacher or Master. My experience on this path has confirmed this perspective. In retrospect, it seems clear to me that a soul that is under the dominion of mind and ego cannot transcend them through his own efforts and guidance. (I use the word "ego" both to refer to that tendency of the mind to elevate oneself above others and the tendency to think of oneself as separate from other people or from the divine, i.e. to be an individual.) One who believes in his own power to free himself must, of course, keep trying. Eventually, he will either succeed or will come to see his helplessness; either outcome would be a step forward. But I was now convinced of the need for help from someone who had made the spiritual transcendence himself.

THE MASTER SPIRITUAL TEACHERS

In order to avoid some misunderstandings about spiritual teachers that confused me as I was learning the teachings at this time, I'd like to explain a few key points now that didn't become clear to me until I had been studying and practicing spirituality for some years. This is not because the Master didn't explain these things, but it took me a long time to understand how he was using some words, to identify what was most important in his teachings, and how all the pieces fit together.

To begin the process of releasing the soul from its imprisonment in the material planes, as described in the previous chapter, a Master gives the initiate some experience of the creative Power that underlies the world. Sant Kirpal Singh said that this is the Power, called *Word* or *Logos* in the Judeo-Christian tradition, *Akash Bani* (voice from the heaven) by the Hindus, or *Bang-i-Ilahi* (call from God) by the Sufis. Every major religion has a different name for this Power, but each name denotes the same real thing. Sant Kirpal Singh Ji often used the words *Shabd* or *Naam,* the terms used in the Sikh scriptures. He had made a deep study of the esoteric teachings of nearly all of the world's major religions, and I was becoming convinced that he had attained firsthand knowledge of the mystic experiences on which those teachings were based. He said this creative Power can be experienced in meditation as inner Light and inner Sound. Some experience of these inner phenomena is given to the student at initiation. The student is asked to increase the experience of the Naam through regular meditation, which is the practice of focusing the attention on the Light and Sound, rather than on the body or sense perceptions or even on thoughts.

The Master takes responsibility for the student's progress, and gives help with many of the karmic burdens that weigh down the soul and bind it to the physical world. Sant Kirpal Singh promised that all initiates, within one or several lifetimes, depending on their spiritual background and discipline, would surely reach the spiritual goal of becoming so absorbed in the Naam or Word that they could truly merge with the creative Power of life, having all their questions answered. I understood little of this theory at the time;

I knew only that I couldn't control my attention or recapture the conscious experiences as I wanted to, and I needed *some* kind of help.

Humans—spiritual entities—can't be wholly satisfied with only material things of the world, and from time to time a soul feels a longing for something closer to her own true nature—something spiritual, and she begins to question, "Who or what am I?" "What do I need in order to be fulfilled?" By oneself, being steeped in lifetimes of forgetfulness, the embodied soul can't answer these questions.

Spiritual teachers say that God sees the plight of humans who have reached this turning point. But God is pure spirit, and humans, having turned their attention to the world and away from spirit, can't hear God speaking. So God commissions an enlightened soul—a soul saturated with divine love and consciousness—to incarnate. As a fellow human being, he comes to the aid of those souls who are questing. We have come to know some of these commissioned souls as those who inspired the great world religions. Each of these spiritual Masters has his list of souls to assist. Each teacher explains things in his own way, a way configured to the needs of the society in which he works. When his assigned tasks are complete, he returns home to God. Another spiritual teacher then takes a place in the world.

I've made no strong distinction between the Master Power overhead—God—and the embodied Master teacher. Indeed, it has been my experience that the divine spiritual consciousness is so transparently represented by the embodied Masters that distinguishing between the two is almost meaningless. As Jesus said, "I and my Father are one." (John 10:30.) For this reason Masters and aspirants alike speak of "Masters" (embodied teachers) and of "*the* Master" (the divine spirit overhead) using the same word, which can be confusing to someone hearing of these teachings for the first time. It's the divine spirit that inspires the student, not the body of the teacher, even when the name that's attached to the body is used at the same time, as in "Master Kirpal." This close association of the physical teacher with the divine Power is the reason that the word "Master" (teacher) is capitalized in Sant Mat literature. The reader will find the same word usage in these pages. The spiritual teachers say that this association of spirit and teacher is an important concept: God speaks and exemplifies the spiritual life through these inspired beings.

The spiritual Master teaches the souls the esoteric nature of life and the method of returning home, which they have forgotten. Then the teacher must reignite divine love in the souls and inspire thoughts and behaviors that make a soul worthy of returning home. In short, he must take a worldly person and make him into a true soul-centered, human being. Only then will the Master guide the soul homeward.

Another of the spiritual teacher's roles is to render the huge account of past stored karmas ineffective. He teaches how to live in a detached manner, allowing the karmas of the present life to work themselves out, while the karmas stored for future lives are rendered ineffective by the spiritual Master himself, like singeing seeds to prevent them from sprouting. The teacher further explains how to meditate, how to transcend body consciousness, which itself burns off the karmas newly generated in the present life. In this way the soul may become free of karma and in a position to experience a joyous homecoming.

The meditation technique used in Sant Mat consists of focusing the attention upon the Naam or Word, the creative Power of life, visible as inner Light and audible as inner Sound. These teachers say that this Power emanates from God and returns to God. So this meditation carries the soul homeward to its source, to God. This technique is simple and yet subtle; it's not something that can be learned from a book. It can be taught only by a master spiritual teacher, through his initiation instructions, and even more through thought transference and eye-to-eye communion. Spiritual teachers seldom speak of the time required to perfect this meditation practice. For a few spiritual students the time can be short, well within a lifetime. But for most students, including myself, many slow personal changes are involved. A lifetime might not be enough. Patience with ourselves is one of the lessons we must learn.

MY INITIATION

Eventually, I felt confident about Master Kirpal and his teachings, and I requested initiation. His acceptance of me was his commitment to take his seat within me, to teach me in many ways, and even to guide my destiny in this life and in the beyond, toward a new relationship with the divine Power overhead—a goal far higher than the goal that I had once set for myself. And my request for initiation was *my* commitment to become a lifelong student of spiritual understanding and self-discipline. I have never regretted this commitment.

My friend at the ashram told me that there is a strong tendency of the mind to avoid the discipline of meditation. The mind, she said, will find a thousand reasons to avoid meditation and, as a result, many people who are initiated give up on spirituality shortly afterwards. She urgently advised me, "David, pray that you may be blessed with the grace of not falling away from this path." She also advised me to attend the *satsangs*, gatherings of initiates in which the teachings are explained, even if I didn't feel like it. My friend said, "Pray." Can a nonreligious person pray? Can he accept the reality of God? Such things are based more on actual inner experience than on blind belief or ritualized worship. It is the awesome experience of the divine, of a numinous presence that touches and communes, that enables prayer, not the outer rituals of institutionalized religion. However, in symbolic form, rituals can also speak to a receptive soul. Numinous experience is not lightly spoken of, even if there were words that were adequate. Only a little such experience can enable prayer. And so, being advised, I took my friend's guidance to heart, and it has served me well throughout life.

I felt a flow of inner help beginning to come my way, and I welcomed it: I sensed the Master's presence within me and a subtle conversation in thought with him. It became a new challenge to me to distinguish between such communications, which I sometimes call "promptings," and my own thoughts. The Master's spiritual presence and these promptings are very real and become quite noticeable as the aspirant progresses. I think it was that very presence in my own heart that manifested itself as the "inner voice" that I have spoken of (chapter 3), and which I had noticed even years before I learned about this spiritual path. The fact of its presence before my initiation suggests to me that I might have been initiated in a past life, maybe more than one past life, in which I learned a little, but not enough to "graduate" from the cycle of earth lives.

The Masters are extremely respectful of their students. They won't push people into accepting initiation, but want them to understand fully what they're committing to. I've heard them urge people to take all the time they want to understand the spiritual path before asking for initiation. I recall the Master saying to one of his students, "Time spent searching is also counted [to one's spiritual credit]." After initiation also, the Masters respect the individual's divinely given free will, even if that is used by the aspirant to slow or block spiritual progress for a time.

My initiation took place in Washington, DC, when I was home for the summer in 1967. A local representative of the Master, an older initiate, had been authorized by the Master to read the initiation instructions to me and to one other person who was to be initiated along with me. The Master does not need to be physically present to give the initiation. According to the Master's teachings, the initiation actually occurs when the Master puts his attention on the aspirant's soul to connect it with the divine Creative Power—the Naam—within. The Master had done this when he accepted me for initiation, even though I was in the US and he was in India at the time. The oral initiation instructions merely provide the aspirant with the theory of the spiritual path and explain how to perform the meditation practices.

In his instructions, the Master briefly described how creation came into being and how the soul, the conscious entity that is one's true self, may experience the Creative Power and even return home to the Creator. The detailed meditation instructions included a mantra of five sacred names. These names, which are spiritually charged by the attention of the Master, are to be repeated mentally—a practice known as *simran*, a Hindi and Punjabi word meaning "remembrance." This repetition helps the aspirant to still the mind's endless flow of thoughts and concentrate the attention one-pointedly within. The spiritual energy that this repetition unleashes also provides the soul with protection from negative influences and eventually acts as a passport to the higher spiritual planes. At my initiation ceremony, as I listened to the Master's meditation instructions, I could feel the Master's attention leading me into meditation. In meditation I had a taste of uplifting spiritual consciousness. Finally, in his closing words, the Master quoted the familiar line from Shakespeare, "This above all: to thine own self be true."[5] I take this to mean that one should be true to that which is most truly oneself: the sacred aspect of oneself. Those quoted words reverberated in my mind and have become a guiding principle to me, as compelling decades later as they were at that time. I left the initiation light-hearted, focused, and happy.

CONFRONTATION WITH THE MIND

After initiation, I put most of the intellectual struggle behind me and found that an even larger task lay ahead: taking the jumble of my mental life in hand and building new patterns of thought and behavior that would be more conducive to a spiritual life. This process was described by the Master as "man-making." It was a matter of becoming true to myself. After the initiation ceremony I went to a movie (which tended to bring my attention to the physical level), and then I went to my parents' home, where for years my life had focused on the physical world. By the next day my spiritual consciousness was gone, and meditation became unappealing. I felt bereaved. But the taste of spiritual consciousness that I had been given at initiation had been even sweeter than the previous experiences, and conscious experience was now becoming necessary to me. I knew that I had suppressed my own spiritual consciousness: through my own choice, or my mental habits, I had run back to more familiar patterns of thought that included a focus on the physical world. Although I felt sad at what I had done to myself, now I better understood how the mind operates, and I was ready to work to regain what I had lost. I had to take control of my mind, steering it away from negative thoughts, and toward a spiritual orientation.

Apparently, many new aspirants go through something similar. Each, in his or her own way, finds it necessary to take control of the mind. But it's no easy task. A large portion of the spiritual teachings are devoted to this subject. To help with this, Sant Kirpal Singh prescribed the daily task of examining one's life, in thought, word, and deed, to establish an ethical base in one's life, a way of life that reflects and respects one's own divine nature. There's a printed form one can use to record these observations, privately. There is even an app for smart phones. He called this exercise "self-introspection." The purpose is to become conscious of one's moral condition—in effect to hold a mirror to oneself. Making a habit of using the self-introspection form was harder than I thought it would be: I felt a rebellion from my mind. But once I did establish that habit, I learned a number of interesting things about myself and my mental life. For instance, I discovered that whenever I do or say something that I later regret, a negative thought or desire almost always comes first. I then tried to recognize such negative thoughts as they arose, using them as an early warning system, giving me a chance to avoid hurting other people. I feel I have avoided much sorrow in this way. I was learning to examine my thoughts, words, and actions as if I were another person, not caring to defend myself against criticism. As I began this introspection, at first it was easy to recognize some of my shortcomings, but after several years I found that there were more subtle negative thoughts, such as fleeting thoughts of superiority, anger, or lust. These brief thoughts were more difficult to recognize as they arose. As one negative thought pattern or desire was laid to rest, other subtler negative patterns or desires rose to the surface to be dealt with in turn, patterns that I had previously been blind to.

One might be able recognize the habits of the mind, which are often attracted to dwell on negative thoughts, but even so, the mind goes on repeating its habits, ignoring the wishes of the aspirant, who tries and fails to bring the mind into order. But in time the mind does come around. I've watched as the numbers on my introspection forms changed over time. My observations of failures would sometimes go up when my perceptions were sharpened, when I learned to see a negative pattern that I hadn't seen before. Then, gradually, they decreased as I learned self-control for that pattern. Overall, I now see the failures approaching, but seldom reaching, zero. For me, such trends take place over decades. Master Kirpal said, "perfection walks slowly."

Following initiation, as I took up the study and practice of spirituality in earnest, I began learning techniques for controlling my negative thoughts and making my words and actions ethical and kind. Being busy with work helped me to change some of the patterns. Sometimes I could do it with a decision: "I don't want to think about this, I'll think about something more positive instead." Sometimes I used the mantra. Another technique that the Master suggested was just to postpone action when one is being tempted: even if the temptation could not be put off indefinitely, I could at least say, "not now." I found that when my own efforts were not enough, prayer, born out of a crying need, often helped to control thoughts and passions in astonishing ways. I found that by controlling my minute-to-minute thoughts, the desires themselves could gradually be quieted, which saved a lot of inner turmoil. At the Master's suggestion, I didn't attempt to eliminate very many personal failings at once: rather, I focused on particular patterns of thought and exerted a steady pressure on my mind to change it over time. I was working to become a true man. It is hard work. The Master said:

> *It is easy for a man to know God,*
> *But to become a man, that is difficult.*[6]

The Master didn't just speak about ethics, but lived ethically himself, all the time, as I could observe, once I met him in person. It was much easier to follow his example than it would have been to adhere to precepts only.

I've often felt that the mind was my enemy, but the Master said the mind could become a friend of the spiritual aspirant and a partner in the soul's spiritual quest. For many years I've been trying to establish such a friendship with my mind, and I feel my mind has come to accept some aspects of the spiritual way of life. However, it has a tendency to rebel, and has never been a reliable friend. Even as I write these pages I feel I'm writing a letter of friendship to my mind. I'm making an effort to express this subject of the heart and soul in words that the mind will understand and appreciate. The Master wrote:

> Mind is no small thing, and is not easy to conquer, but we should start by changing its direction. While its face remains turned toward the worldly things, the soul will be worldly, but if it turns around and faces the soul, the soul will become spiritual. We must turn it around. Like fire, it is a good servant but a bad master.[7]

The ethical failings that I and many others have in our lives are not matters for self-flagellation or depression. I see them as simply the human condition of souls who have endured lifetimes under the dominion of mind in an iron-hard material world. For the spiritual aspirant they are things that must be transcended, and the first step in this is recognizing that these failings exist. Those who have faced and acknowledged their own shortcomings will be less inclined to criticize others and will have more humility and forgiveness. One trembles to see oneself as others see one, but that's the challenge before the spiritual aspirant. Seeing one's own faults might be the hardest part. I also saw that other aspirants had faults that apparently they didn't see in themselves. Having discovered some of my own blindness, I wondered how many more faults in myself I was also blind to. It became more difficult to criticize others who erred, when I became convinced that I, too, might err blindly.

A PHOTOGRAPH OF HAZUR

The Master told us that photos of the Master are only meant for remembrance and not for other purposes. (I think he was speaking of divination, idolatry, or wish fulfillment, etc.) Here is a story of how I used such a picture in a way that the Master might not have approved of and what I learned from the experience.

In the late 1960's, about two years after I was initiated by Sant Kirpal Singh, I lived near Boston and attended satsang there. I hadn't yet met Master Kirpal in person, but his teachings spoke strongly to me, and I could see something divine even in his photographs. In our satsang meetings there were photos of Master Kirpal and his Master, Hazur Baba Sawan Singh (1858–1948), whom I knew little about, in the front of the room every Sunday. The photo of Hazur troubled me because I was never able to see any divinity in his photo, as I could in the photos of Master Kirpal. From other aspirants I had also heard stories of the Masters actually coming alive in photographs, even of stepping out of the picture and greeting people. I take it that these were spontaneous visionary experiences: if another person had been looking at the photo at the same time, they would not necessarily have seen that change. I felt that to ask for some visionary experience related to a photo was not appropriate, but my desire for understanding was strong. I had heard that the Masters were very kind and had a forgiving sense of humor. So I didn't feel shy about asking for some kind of experience to help me understand this "granddaddy" spiritual teacher.

One Sunday, when the satsang had concluded, and people were leaving, I, in a calm spirit of scientific inquiry, walked up to Hazur's photograph and focused my attention on it. Almost immediately that photograph changed for a moment—I kid you not—into the image of my very own face. I don't think the Master was rebuking me—rather, he was respectfully and humorously conveying through thought transference that at the level of soul we are one. He actually seemed to be placing himself at my own level, pointing out a potential on my part that I hadn't realized. I was astounded and humbled. I recognized the humor, but I didn't laugh. I said to Hazur, "Thank you; I understand." Since that time, I have never again felt the need to ask a photograph to speak to me in this way, and none ever has. Neither have I had to question again the humble divinity of Hazur Baba Sawan Singh. And I saw for myself that the Masters do have a keen sense of humor. The young aspirant was learning through many experiences.

LIFE IN THE WORLD

These efforts in understanding, in self-introspection, and in trying to meditate in stillness were at the center of my spiritual life for many years. I had a worldly life too: after my undergraduate degree I worked first as a draftsman in Boston, then I pursued a master's degree at the University of North Carolina at Chapel Hill, which led to jobs teaching high school chemistry and physics. Later, I became a remodeling contractor. In all these jobs I strove to fairly serve my employers, my students, my construction customers, and to kindly teach skills to my construction employees. I didn't become wealthy, nor did I expect to. The Master had said, "A completely honest man can barely afford to keep body and soul together." I was able to meet the financial needs of a simple life that didn't demand many luxuries. But my spiritual values were a priority.

Spiritual teachers say that the world of our physical lives is a mere passing show, mostly for our education. Whatever we experience can inform us of values, of what is worth having or doing. We take nothing with us from this life except what we learn at the level of soul: that understanding which becomes a part of us. Otherwise, what should we care about this theater of images? It became my resolve to live so lightly in the world that challenges and setbacks wouldn't upset me. But after five years of effort in meditation and self-introspection, I still felt I had barely begun my spiritual pursuit. It was not until I met Sant Kirpal Singh in person that my spiritual goals became focused and even more urgent.

Look Ma—no hands!
One foot on shore, my other tilts the boat.
You sit onboard so calmly, hand held out.
But don't help me. I can do this by myself.

I didn't see the rolling wave,
Or was it the shore that heaved?
How was I to know
I'd land face down in mud?

You wash my face so patiently,
My clothes are soiled, yes.
More laundry—but what are mothers for?
Now let me go; I want to play.

Night comes, you say—we must go home,
But the evening air is fine.
There are paths to run and trees to climb.
Our picnic island is a paradise.

But now it's night, and I am tired,
Dark shadows seem to roam.
This island world has lost its charm.
Please take my hand, and let's go home.

CHAPTER SIX

Ocean of Love

1972

I first met Sant Kirpal Singh in 1972, at Dulles Airport, near Washington, DC, as he arrived in America on a world speaking tour. The events of that day shook my life to its foundation.

Some 200 people gathered at the airport to greet him, most of us for the first time. I had put a lot of hope in the ability of this Master to help me grow spiritually. In anticipation of the meeting, I asked myself many questions: Would he somehow be too big for me? Or would he prove to be no more than another ego-bound individual at my own level? How could I even know? If he were the spiritual Master that I took him to be, how would he respond to me? Had I grown spiritually during the five years since I had received initiation? I didn't know any of the answers.

The people waiting for the Master were quiet, many sitting with eyes closed in the airport lounge. Some talked softly, and one group sang lovely devotional songs. After more than an hour of waiting, someone announced that the Master's plane had landed, but that he still had to go through customs. We waited.

At last, a door opened into the lounge, and the Master walked toward us, smiling. Some of the organizers greeted him first, then he turned toward the rest of us. With hands together in deep respect, he greeted each person individually with his eyes. He seldom spoke, and we were silent.

When he came to me, he looked into my eyes, and I saw into his. His eyes were wide open with a simplicity and innocence that one sees occasionally in small children. Then something happened that I hadn't anticipated: his eyes grew deep. I saw into the Master's very being, and I found that inside he was a whole world of nothing but love—a living Ocean of Love that invited me to plunge into it. It was beautiful! It was everything I had hoped for—more than I had hoped for. I was awed by what I saw. My mind stood silent.

What I was seeing was visionary. This was seeing, not with physical vision but with the vision of the soul. There *is* such a thing! This was my first experience of *darshan*, of relating to a spiritual teacher through his eyes. No one had prepared me for this. Probably there is no such thing as being prepared for this. As will be seen, experiences of darshan became a regular feature of my spiritual pursuit.

But as I looked into the Master's eyes, there came a crisis that has shaped the rest of my life. If I could go back and change only one event in my whole life, it might be that moment. My fearful mind rose up in protest, literally saying to me, "Wait a minute, this is all too fast!" My mind took control; my gaze withdrew from the Master, and something like a shutter closed in my vision. I found myself seeing only the surface of the Master's face again. I was deeply disturbed about that fear, and I thought, "What am I here for!" The Master had been showing me his innermost self—I felt that the Ocean of Love still beckoned to me—and I had refused it! The Master still was looking at me, and his eyes were inviting. I think he understood the conflict I was undergoing, hoping that I might recover my spiritual vision. Quickly, I focused my attention on him again, but still I could see only the surface of his face. Then he was greeting the person next to me. Desperately, I called with my mind, "Please come back!" But by then he was even farther away.

I watched in longing silence while he greeted every other person in the room, and then he strode out to a waiting car. The people began milling around, some smiling, some with tears flowing down their cheeks. A friend told me that some people wearing airport uniforms had stunned looks on their faces or tears in their eyes. The Master had silently greeted them also.

LESSONS LEARNED

My vision in the Master's eyes was an experience in which the soul learned through direct experience. No thought, no mental rationalization was involved. It was certain knowledge: no argument could change it. I had no idea that the Master could affect me so profoundly, or that he could touch the hearts of so many people in such a short time. Clearly, this man had a deep spiritual connection, and he could communicate it to others. I no longer doubted that he was a spiritual Master. But the discovery of my own fear and the power of my ego-ridden mind to close off my eye-to-eye communion with the Master shocked me. What had I been afraid of? Slowly, it became plain that love itself in pure selfless form called me to inculcate within myself an equal purity and selflessness, and I didn't have that purity. My soul was ashamed of her filthy condition. She wished to conceal herself. (Soul is often given the feminine gender in mystic teachings.) Indeed, my mental life was full of impurity: anger, lust, greed, and self-importance. How could I possibly enter that Ocean of Love and remain there? I now saw with painful clarity that my main job in life could only be somehow to overcome the hardness of my mind, to grow until I no longer needed the "shutter" in my vision that came between my Master and me. "Sometime," I thought soberly, "sometime, maybe, I'll be able to take that plunge in the Ocean of Love, but I'm a long way from being ready now." The Master had told us that such an inner transformation was necessary, but I hadn't realized how urgent or what an immense job it would be. Decades later, I still struggle to make that transformation, to bring my inner and outer life into consonance with that promised divine connection. The Master often succinctly said, "Time factor is a necessity."

I've just spoken about the soul as being distinct from the mind, and I should make that distinction clear. In the days I'm describing, I couldn't have clearly differentiated mind and soul. Like the psychologists, of whom I've complained, I confused these two states of awareness. As I write, half a century later, I find I can now more clearly express that distinction: "Mind," as my teachers use the word, is a faculty that thinks mostly in emotions, words, images, or symbols. Its task is to make some sense of the world around it, whether that world is physical or mental. Mind, being by nature less conscious than the creative Power overhead, is not equipped to perceive reality in full, in spite of the fascinating discoveries of the particle physicists. If the mind has consciousness, then it's something borrowed or appropriated from the soul. The soul, on the other hand, is a thing of consciousness, the home of consciousness in the human being. It is soul that gives life and consciousness to humans. Soul is the real "I"—to the extent that "I" is real at all. Soul experiences reality directly. It needs no words, images or symbols. Soul is something seldom experienced in its essence by humans, as it speaks much more quietly than the mind. Soul is drowned out by the torrent of thoughts from the mind. Soul is experienced directly only when the mind becomes still, which is seldom. The spiritual path that I follow stresses the familiar maxim: *Man, know thyself.* That is an injunction to experience the soul in its essence and therefore to learn how to still the mind.

As I walked out of the airport, a thought came to me. It was surely an inner message, a prompting, from my spiritual Master's thoughts. It asked me to consider the Greek legend of the Fifth Labor of Hercules—*The Cleaning of the Augean Stables.*[8] I recognized the symbolism: the stables surely represent the mind, which had just mocked me with its dirt. But what was symbolized by the two rivers that Hercules used to clean the stables? Perhaps they represent the inner Light and Sound Currents that I could experience in meditation, and, as in the legend, those currents alone could do much of the work. Could it really be that simple?

At the airport I had become distressed by the discovery of the negative power of my mind. But my Master had not left me alone to suffer. He had now told me how to overcome the negative tendencies of the mind. And that was on top of giving me my first experience of darshan, which showed me something of the depth that a human being might attain when the spiritual side of life is developed. And I had become aware of the side of myself that opposed the spiritual progress that I desired. In a matter of moments I had learned several deep lessons of spirituality.

When I first wrote about this incident, shortly after it occurred, and metaphorically titled it "Ocean of Love" in an effort to describe my experience, I was unaware that no less a personage than Kabir had used the same imagery, which became the title of one of his most important compositions, the *Anurag Sagar,*[9] (translated as *The Ocean of Love*) a book-length spiritual poem, among the earliest descriptions of Sant Mat, dating to half a millennium ago. The fact that the same metaphor came to my mind suggests to me that my experience in darshan was part of a long-standing spiritual tradition.

The hardness of the mind, like an arctic iceberg cold,
Breaking from its ancient glacier mold,
Floating south toward the luring tropic clime
Melts in many tears of love divine.
Soul asks, looking upward in devotion,
"Are we not the essence of the Ocean?"

CHAPTER SEVEN

Human Unity[10]

1974

As people begin to explore the spiritual side of life they begin to transcend race, nationality, and culture, all of which are associated with the body and the outer world. The meaning and wonder of being human opens up, and they begin to appreciate who and what they are as spiritual beings, to appreciate that other people are similar in nature, and that there is a divine connection between all of us.

To encourage such inquiry, Master Kirpal organized a number of World Fellowship of Religions conferences, inviting leaders of various faiths to sit together and consider ways to find religious unity at the spiritual level. This was well before interfaith conferences became popular. In the last year of his life, Master Kirpal made his appeal even broader, organizing a unity conference oriented not toward organized religions, but toward mankind in general. Its purpose was to find ways in which ordinary people might discover their spiritual unity with all of humanity—to follow "a ray of hope for human regeneration." It was the first time in centuries that a spiritual leader had sponsored a conference that focused on this subject. He called this the *Conference on the Unity of Man*, and it was held in Delhi, India, in February, 1974, two years after I first met him in person near Washington, DC. (When the spiritual Master used the word "man," it was generally in the classic sense, meaning "human.") It became the largest unity conference that he had sponsored. Tens of thousands of people attended, mostly from India. About 600 people came from other countries around the world. This conference was a good setting for my first trip to India. I attended in response to an open invitation that was read at our meetings in the United States, but a strong *inner* call coming to me at the same time made me know that I must go to India for this conference. I gave thought to what I might say to this assembly concerning spiritual human unity, but I soon realized that I knew too little to make any contribution at all. I thought there was spiritual meaning in this theme—implying more than simple social fairness or compassion, but I couldn't grasp that meaning or put it in words. Still, I did wish to learn, and at the conference that wish was granted.

A huge tent gave shelter from the sun. The speakers' dais was a simple raised platform that held some fifty people. The audience sat cross-legged on thin carpeting that covered the ground. The conference sessions lasted eight to ten hours a day, for four days. A few of the talks were in English, but most were in Hindi or other languages I didn't understand, and few were translated. Still, this conference became one of the watershed events of my life.

The Master took a limited role in these unity conferences, being only one of the many speakers. During the conference he left organizational matters to others. He spoke about once a day. In the keynote speech of the conference, titled "The Remodeling of Our Destiny," he said:

> The problem before us is how to bring about a change in man's heart and effect his inner conversion so that

> he can see truly and clearly and learn to discriminate between truth and untruth. Since this lies beyond the scope of body and intellect, it can only come about through an inward illumination of divine wisdom in the sanctuary of the soul.
>
> This is the individual aspect of the matter. We also have to forge abiding bonds of kinship among the nations of the world so that they will treat each other with genuine courtesy based on inward love and friendliness, and seek the welfare of all members of the human family, transcending their political ideologies which create rivalries and international tensions.[11]

Dozens of speakers addressed the subject of human unity, each in his or her own way. Some of the speakers were well known, such as Sufi Pir Vilayat Inayat Khan and Indian Prime Minister Indira Gandhi. Other speakers represented various countries and regions, including India, North America, Europe, Africa, Australia, the Middle East, and the Far East.

Sant Kirpal Singh was nearly always present on the crowded dais. During the talks he silently watched the people in the audience, his eyes moving from one person to another. Sometimes his eyes would stop and his attention would be fixed on one person for some seconds. I'd experienced those expressive eyes when I first met the Master two years before at the airport near Washington, DC (previous chapter), and I wondered what experiences he might be giving to those people on whom his eyes came to rest. I felt magnetically drawn to his eyes and face, and I felt they revealed something of what he had become through his pursuit of spirituality. It became my main occupation to try to read this profound "book" of spirituality sitting quietly before us.

A VISION IN HIS EYES

I saw the human level—his beautiful expression, a light in his face, a sparkle in his eyes—but there was something even deeper, beyond words. After days of this watching, I began to see more than a human being in the face of the Master. I had a second glimpse of that "Ocean of Love." The Master's attention must have been directed toward me at this moment, but I was aware only of that spiritual vision in his eyes. I could see that a divine presence was before me. He was building a bridge of love, of consciousness, between the two of us, from eye to eye. I longed to escape from my body, to emerge onto the bridge and meet him face to face. It was an unspoken prayer.

Then I found something within myself responding to the Master's divinity—something that went out in love to meet this special person—something in me that was of a similar nature to his, and I experienced a newly awakened consciousness or movement of love within myself. This consciousness took its place behind my eyes and remained there. I was able to sustain my eye-to-eye contact longer than I was at my first meeting with him. For me it was a wonderful encounter both with the Master and with the spiritual side of my own being, which I hadn't met before to this extent. That meeting of eyes, of hearts, seemed to last for a long time—a timeless time.

Not long after this, the conference broke for a midday meal, which was served right in the tent. Most members of the audience stood to stretch their legs, and I, too, walked about. I still carried this new consciousness, my own sparkle in my eyes, and I felt very happy. Until then, I hadn't paid much attention to the other people at the conference, but now I looked about. I knew that my consciousness would be visible through my eyes to someone else who had had a similar experience. A man walked toward me, an Indian, and his eyes were shining. I saw that he, too, had this consciousness, or had been touched in the same way, and he could see it in me. We responded to each other with a smile of recognition and then with shared laughter of delight. We met very wonderfully, speaking only eye-to-eye, heart-to-heart, and I liked him immediately.

Then a thought came to me (that I am sure came from that Master Power overhead), which directed me to sit down and think about the meaning of human unity. I hadn't understood it when I first came to this conference, but I had wished to understand. Now, having recognized this divine consciousness in my Master, in myself, and in another man, I easily understood that this same consciousness, or at least the potential for it, is in every person alive on the earth, even if it is deeply buried—as it had been in me. Further, I thought that such divine consciousness all came from the same source. That aspect of consciousness that is shared by us all is what I've come to understand as God. Intuitively, I understood that this consciousness is one entity, the central aspect of existence, which also had a presence within each individual. Seen in that light, individuals cannot be separate, but are united by that spiritual Power. It's at that conscious level, the spiritual level, that we are one, and that was the experiential understanding of human unity that I gained at this conference. If enough people could make this discovery, the Master explained, it would change the world, even at the political level.

I think it was the fact that my attention was directed to my spiritual teacher that this clarity came to mind. It was, of course, not an original idea with me, nor even original with my teacher, but was a concept that has been expressed repeatedly by great thinkers throughout history. This was another experience of learning at the level of soul. Indeed, most of my experiences with Master Kirpal, and with those spiritual teachers who came after him, have had this kind of learning involved, often with intellectual explanations added, to help me understand what was being taught.

I thought, "Isn't this essentially the same message that's at the heart of Christianity and, for that matter, every other major religion?" It was also essentially the same conclusion I had come to when I was exploring the theory of spirituality at Goddard College (chapter 4). It was important for me to approach this subject from many angles, finding that different perspectives all led to the same conclusion. It was a wonder to me that I had found a teacher who could help me and many others to grow in consciousness and grasp this deep understanding through his words, his example, his eye-to-eye communication, but also through our own first-hand experience. I was beginning to consider this way of learning as the *only* way to fully learn anything. This very practical lesson was formative to me, further deepening my spiritual urgency.

At the end of the Unity of Man Conference, confirming my understanding in his concluding remarks, the Master said:

> The fact is that unity already exists—we have forgotten it. What is that unity? The right understanding that all men are born in the same way with the same privileges from God and the same construction outside and inside. As man we are all one—no high, no low. . . . We are one at the level of that [divine] conscious entity which is administering this factory [complex physical mechanism] of the human body. So we are conscious beings and God is all conscious.[12]

What makes a man worthy of respect?
Stylish clothes, a limousine, a snappy uniform?
Those things are not him at all.

The color of his skin, his place of birth, his public words?
No, these might not reflect his being.
Where—where?—is the man worthy of respect?

To find the man, see who is peeping from his eyes.
Or does he hide his eyes,
With arrogance—or fear?
Can we see the real man behind the mask he wears?
Greet him with a kindly smile to call the real man forth.
There—there!—is the man worthy of respect.

CHAPTER EIGHT

Meditation at Sawan Ashram

1972

Meditation is a practice that is fundamental to the spiritual quest. When I attended the Unity of Man Conference, even though it had been seven years since my initiation, I was still very much a beginner in meditation, as I still take myself to be today. So the meditation lessons that were coming to me were beginning lessons.

I was one of a large group of people who had arrived on the same flight from America and Europe. We arrived by bus at Sawan Ashram, where Master Kirpal lived and met with thousands of visitors from India and abroad. The spiritual Master met with us in the courtyard just outside the gate of his house. He embraced many of us, welcoming his children from far away. My memory paints the scene in colors of love. "You are at home here," he said. Since we had arrived a week before the conference was to start, he asked that during this week we devote four to six hours a day to prayerful meditation. "You have nothing else to do!" he said with a smile. But in America I couldn't sit still and meditate even for two-and-a-half hours a day, as he asked us to do, so I was sure I'd fail to meet his expectation. However, when I meditated in the charged atmosphere of the ashram, I found the sittings a pleasure, and I was able to sit for long periods. Then, I tried to find all the time I could for meditation.

One day, I noticed a young man standing still in the courtyard just outside my dormitory room with eyes nearly closed, apparently lost in reverie. An hour or two later, walking past, I saw him again, sitting in a chair near where I had seen him before. Now his eyes were closed, but his head was upright. Several young initiates were gathered about him, and one lady (I was told she was a group leader) reached out and gently shook his leg and then his shoulder. He did not respond in any way. Evidently he had completely withdrawn from physical consciousness. He seemed almost dead. That lady told the others that this was what was meant by the Master's injunction to "die while living." I was struck by the realization that such deep meditation is possible.

During the weeks before and after the conference, the Master often met with the Westerners. He attentively asked for our questions, frequently telling the questioner, "Come here, please." Then that person would come to the front, and the Master would talk to him or her heart-to-heart while the others also enjoyed the sweet interchange. Under a tree or in the meditation building, he would talk to us about meditation and give us instructions as we began to meditate. After an hour or so he would return and gently say, "Leave off, please." Then he would ask us to report our inner experiences with a show of hands. He would ask who had seen flashes of Light. . . the starry sky. . . the inner sun. . . the moon. . . as well as other inner visions. He would have the hands counted, and with his fountain pen he wrote the numbers on a folded piece of paper that he carried with him, a little like a scientist writing in his laboratory notebook.

Once he told us about an Indian aspirant who was fond of meditating in train stations, where there were always crowds of people, bustle, and noise. This aspirant, he explained, considered that all the activity had nothing to do with him, and the busy people ignored his presence, so he felt quite cut off from the activity, alone in meditation. We were to understand from this that if we controlled our attention in this way, then meditation was possible in nearly all circumstances.

THE STUDENT IS TESTED

Another day, he gave us the same lesson in a different way. On that day, many carpenters were working in the meditation building, separated from us only by a thin curtain. While the Master gave the meditation instructions, we could hear hammering and sawing echoing throughout the hall. In those days I worked as a carpenter myself, and I took much interest in the efficient but labor-intensive manual methods that the carpenters used in India. When the Master finished the meditation instructions, we sat still with eyes closed. The noise from the carpenters intruded on my awareness. I wondered what they were making. With annoyance, I asked myself why we had to share this noisy space during our meditation time. But I was not meditating.

As usual, when the sitting was over, the Master asked for a show of hands to indicate what our inner experiences had been. We found that most people had meditated successfully in spite of the noise, but more than usual had, like me, been distracted. The Master compared the numbers to those from previous days on his folded piece of paper and appeared to be perplexed. Focusing on those of us who had had no inner experience, he pressed us to tell him why we had not been able to meditate properly this time. Someone said, "I couldn't meditate because of all the noise."

Perhaps the Master was waiting for such a remark. That was when he gave us a serious lecture, saying that after all his coaching we had been given a test. He told us again that meditation is an *inner* practice, and the noise was only an outer thing. We had nothing to do with the carpenters, and they had nothing to do with us, so we could ignore this noise. I learned that there may always be noises around us, always things that will interest us if we let them draw our attention, but when we sit for meditation, we are to be quite divorced from the body and everything around us. The spiritual Master taught us in so many ways.

It's mind that fears the darkness,
It's mind that fears the Light.
Mind fears to lose its rule supreme,
But soul fears nothing mind can dream.
To soul, the Light brings life.

In challenge to the darkness,
Light of higher realms shines bright,
Soul reaches for that vision, its desire.
I welcome soul's new wisdom and inquire,
"Am I not a child of Light?"

See that Light, let it be;
Be that Light, it is me.

PART 3

Years with Sant Darshan Singh Ji

CHAPTER NINE

Searching for the New Master

1974–75

At the time of the Unity of Man Conference, in February 1974, Sant Kirpal Singh was 80 years old. He had lived a strenuous life of service, the last 26 years as a public figure. He was not in good health. I thought that he would be preparing a successor to shoulder the task of initiating and guiding the thousands of people who were drawn to this spiritual path each year, and while I was at the conference I decided to find out, if I could, who that successor was by carefully observing each of the speakers.

While I sat in the conference, day after day, I watched dozens of people come to the podium. There were many guest speakers and many more speakers who worked closely with Master Kirpal. I thought, "This is the biggest conference the Master has sponsored, and that successor *must* be here." One of the most remarkable features of Master Kirpal was the radiance that I could sometimes see in his face and eyes that revealed his highly developed consciousness. So I decided I'd look for that radiance in each of the speakers. I also used my intuition just at the level of understanding. But nearly all the people who addressed us seemed to me to be ordinary people who exhibited varying degrees of ego. A few of the speakers kept their inner natures shielded somehow, and I couldn't see into them. In not one speaker could I see a sign of the Master's degree of consciousness. On the last day of the conference, when the featured speeches were over and many people were leaving, I was ready to admit defeat.

Then, when the program was all over, I noticed that the Master had moved to the back of the dais where he sat, nearly hidden, beside his son, Darshan. They were engaged in animated conversation. Finally, I saw what I had been looking for: both their faces were lit up with divine radiance, love, and joy. I said to myself, "They are two of a kind!" I had perhaps found a clue to the puzzle. Darshan had been one of the speakers whom I had not been able to see into. Was he to be the next Master? But I let the question go after this—I was in no rush to think of my Master's death.

WHEN A SPIRITUAL MASTER DIES

Only six months later, we got the news of the Master's passing. It was a terrible blow to the aspirants. It is said that the bond of love between a Master and an aspirant was not subject to death, and that after his death the aspirant could feel his Master's presence just as strongly. This bond of love with the Master, of which we now became so painfully aware, is central to the teachings of this line of spiritual teachers. Our elder brother and sister aspirants told us that it is through this love connection with such a rare, fully God-realized person, who has transcended his ego, that initiates can link themselves to God. When such a Master is found, it can lead to rapid spiritual growth. But *finding* such a person is fraught with difficulties. The Master had taught that at least one such person is always on the earth, but as best I could determine, Master Kirpal had not announced who his successor was to be.

Many of the aspirants of my acquaintance sought out whichever possible successor who seemed right to each.

Before long, several people claimed that Master Kirpal had given them his spiritual mantle, and some people were following each one. Few of the Westerners, mostly novices like me, could say with certainty—from inner experience—who Master Kirpal had entrusted with the task of initiating new seekers into the meditation practice: that is, whom we could look to as a teacher and guide. After my view of the Master and his son together at the Unity Conference, I felt I had been given a clue, and sure enough, most of the initiates in India were turning to the Master's son, now referred to as Sant Darshan Singh Ji. But I thought I shouldn't look to a new teacher without more evidence of his competency than just the one revealing sight I had had of him then. It's difficult, if not impossible, for a novice spiritual aspirant to truly measure a Master. A realized man won't boast or show off his inner abilities, but will behave humbly and live simply. The aspirant, with outer eyes and intellectual judgment alone, might not be able to see the Master's inner awakening—his consciousness—or his ability to awaken others. Still, sometimes the Master himself, or the Master overhead, finds a way to show who and what he is to an aspirant who urgently wishes to know.

RETURN TO INDIA[13]

One of the Master's representatives in America, Mr. T.S. Khanna, had organized a group trip to India, vigorously challenging the initiates to see for themselves what happened when one Master passed and another took up the role. I was moved by his challenge, and I joined that group flight. It was August 1975, one year after the Master's passing, and a public commemoration, a *bhandara*, was to be held. Sant Darshan Singh would meet with the Westerners who came, and he would participate in the events. On the plane, I wrote down several criteria by which I might recognize a Master, characteristics that were unique to Master Kirpal, such as his profound humility, his ability to give darshan (the experience of divinity through his eyes), his own life being an example of the teachings, and his ability to awaken inner experience in others. I felt that my efforts were necessary, that I was responsible for my choice of a teacher. But I also saw that my judgement was subject to error because of my limited perceptions. Soon I closed my notebook, thinking that if he only would, a new Master would just have to show himself to me in his own way. (I should explain that "darshan" is an ancient Sanskrit word, meaning "seeing," which is used in Sant Mat to indicate the eye-to-eye communion with a spiritual teacher. And now, this word, used as his given name, seemed a portent of the role Sant Darshan Singh was taking on.)

We arrived at the airport in Delhi, India, at 5:30 a.m. As our group went through customs, the sun rose brightly. I was carrying boxes of books and supplies to our bus when I noticed a hush around me. I turned and saw Sant Darshan Singh only a few feet away with a small group close around him. I never expected him to meet us at the airport! His hands were together in the traditional Indian greeting, and his eyes were very intense. How slowly and deliberately he moved from one person to another! Then, thinking of the criteria I had written during the flight, I began to ask myself whether he was meeting my expectations, whether I could see the divine radiance, and whether I could receive darshan from him, and then of course, because I was relying on my intellect, I stopped really seeing him. He greeted me with a nod and a glance, but my mind was busy, and I was not receptive to the subtler things. For all my effort, I had missed my chance to really see him. More people from our group were gathering around, and I felt I could see the same questions and anxieties in their eyes that I was feeling. But some were very receptive: tears ran down their cheeks. There was a young man with us who looked awe-stricken and sobered, like I had felt when I first met Sant Kirpal Singh. This young man was not even an initiate. I thought, "So *some* people are receiving darshan from him—if only it could be me!"

Sant Darshan Singh had no ashram in those days, so the Indian initiates rented several large, modern houses for the Western visitors. During the two weeks that most of us stayed in India, the Master frequently met with us at one of these houses, in the living room, on the rooftop, or in the courtyard. He seemed to be a very simple man. He was very loving and considerate of our comfort and welfare. Sometimes things he said reminded me of Master Kirpal. Such things would catch in my heart, and a deep, painful longing would arise. I hadn't known that love could be so painful, but perhaps I should have known: Master Kirpal had once said to a small group of us, "When love dances on the heart, it causes pain."

One evening, shortly after sunset, as the overwhelming heat of the day gave way to coolness and semidarkness, Master Darshan met with us Westerners in the courtyard of the house. He talked about Master Kirpal as he remembered him. No one asked the question directly, but Master Darshan seemed to be aware of our anxiety over accepting a new Master. As he spoke, I felt he was trying to open himself to us, to let us know who he was, and he was inviting us to ask our anxious questions.

Finally, one of the Western aspirants spoke for many of us by telling him, "I feel love for you, but it's not the same as I felt for Master Kirpal. This new love can't take the place of the old." Master Darshan replied with great feeling, saying, in effect: You are right. No one will ever take the place of your own Master. His passing leaves a wound that can never really heal in the initiate's heart. Then he recited a verse by the Urdu poet Ghalib, then explained it in English. The poet was complaining that his beloved, through her eyes, with their bow-shaped brows, had pierced him with a "half-drawn arrow." It had not gone all the way through his heart, making an end of the matter, but *lodged* in his heart, causing lasting pain. That, Master Darshan said, is the condition of the spiritual lover. Then he told us, "This is a path of love, and we have all been struck by such a half-drawn arrow."

His answer acknowledged the empty place in our hearts and in no way asked us to accept him as our Master, but rather as a brother aspirant. Here, and in other conversations, he presented himself on our own level, as someone who is struggling to live up to the expectations of his own Master, as we were. He made no claim to any ability, saying that it was the Master *overhead* who had touched us within, and it was only that spiritual Power that could inspire the aspirants. While saying this, he made a gesture that I later saw him make many times when he spoke of the Master "overhead." He touched his forehead, then pointed upward and looked upward, and his liquid eyes actually seemed to see that transcendental Master "overhead." The humility that he expressed during this meeting, and others, showed me that this Master's life *was* an example of the spiritual teachings, one of the criteria I had written down.

THE BHANDARA

The bhandara, the death anniversary observance, was to last for three days, August 20–22. Like most large gatherings in India, it took place under a big tent, an expanse of colorful awnings, laced together and supported by many poles, the purpose of which was only to give shelter from the hot sun. When we Westerners visited the meeting grounds the day before the program started, there was tenting overhead, but it had rained, and there were mud puddles everywhere under the tent. Twenty or thirty Indians, doing humble service out of love for the Master, scooped the dirty water from the puddles into buckets with their bare hands. Then they spread dry carpeting for everyone to sit on.

On the first day of the program the dais was mostly bare wood, very plain. It was an appropriate setting, as a feeling of grief and loss pervaded. The faces of the people were long. The speeches reflected the burden of bereavement. Even the sky gently wept under dark gray clouds. Sant Darshan Singh sat on the dais. He strongly reminded me of Master Kirpal, his eyes roving among the people, seldom blinking, his presence seeming to contradict our very grief. Several thousand Indian devotees were present. Many of them must have had questions about the authenticity of the new Master, just as we Westerners did.

The second day, the actual anniversary of Master Kirpal's passing, was quite different. The dais was decorated with bunting and flowers. On this day some twenty or thirty yogis from the valley of the River Ganges and other religious leaders came to confer their recognition of Sant Darshan Singh as Master Kirpal's true successor, calling him "The king of saints." I recognized many of them as having been speakers at the Unity of Man Conference in 1974. As a Hindu symbol of their recognition, they tied a colored string bracelet around Sant Darshan Singh's wrist, and garlanded him with flowers. Also, the yogis presented him with a small brass urn of water from the Ganges, a traditional offering for yogis to make to a holy man. The Ganges has sacred significance in India, and Master Kirpal's ashes had been placed in the Ganges after his death. Because of this, while Master Darshan was holding up the urn for all to see, one of the yogis, Swami Ved Vyasanand, with eyes sparkling, and with a sweeping flourish of his arm, jovially announced in English, "Sant Kirpal Singh Ji is in that pot!" But I was watching Master Darshan's eyes, and at last I saw the divine power in them. I thought, "No. Sant Kirpal Singh Ji isn't in that pot. He's in those eyes!" Now I knew that this Master could give darshan, another of the criteria I had written. At the height of this ceremony, heavy rain suddenly started to fall, which was considered an outward sign of divine blessing. A few minutes later, the rain ended abruptly, just as the ceremony concluded, lending cosmic weight to what had seemed at first to be only a man-made ceremony.

THE TURBAN CEREMONY

Until recently, among Sikhs in India it was customary, and is still observed by some families, that when a man who is head of a household or extended family dies, usually the eldest son takes up his role. A ceremony is held in which the deceased father's turban is tied on the son's head to symbolize this transition of responsibility and authority. How heavy that turban must feel to the younger man! Master Darshan was the eldest living son of Master Kirpal, but this ceremony hadn't yet been held for him. On this second day of the bhandara, some leaders had arranged that the turban-tying ceremony would be held as not just a family affair, but on the dais, before the assembled aspirants. Sant Darshan Singh Ji was seated, cross-legged on the floor, in the middle of the large dais. While the preliminary talks were being given, I was blessed once more by being able to see the divinity in his eyes. His eyes were two orbs of serenity, unmoved and far above all the excitement on the dais. His face, too, now looked just like Master Kirpal's. I looked more carefully, thinking that I must be seeing wrongly, but the more I focused my attention on him, the more complete this transformation became. I was sitting close enough to see clearly. I thought that his face must have physically changed. Indeed he *was* Master Kirpal for me in a real sense, familiar and loving, with the full power of the Master within. Gratitude welled up in my heart that I might have this nearness to my Master one more time. Tears came to my eyes. This vision lasted throughout the entire turban ceremony.

To our surprise, when the ceremonial turban was presented on the dais, it turned out not to be one of Master Kirpal's (his father's), but was a turban that had belonged to the great Hazur Baba Sawan Singh (1858–1948), the Master of both Master Kirpal and Master Darshan. I heard a loud collective gasp as the Indian devotees grasped the daring symbolism: this was to be a dramatic affirmation of Master Darshan's new role as spiritual teacher—as a Master. The Indian devotees stood up and made a tumult of approval as the turban of the "Great Saint of Beas" was slowly wound over Sant Darshan Singh's own turban. Many leaders lent a hand, each taking one or two turns of the turban cloth. All this time I saw Master Kirpal's eyes and face before me in the face of Sant Darshan Singh.

In the middle of this excitement on the dais, thunder rolled and rain poured down again, coming right through the tent. The spirits of the Indian devotees soared, as they regarded the rain as a blessing from—even as the spiritual presence of—the great Hazur Baba Sawan Singh, whose turban and authority were being passed on. (Hazur was born in and named after the fourth month in the Hindu calendar—Sawan—beginning in late July and ending in the third week of August, a period also known as "the month of rains," during which the arrival of the monsoon deluges heat-stricken northern India with heavy rainfall, to the delight of the people.) Someone shouted, "Let it rain!" And it did rain, hard. Some people were utterly drenched, and their faces were filled with light and joy. Among the Indians, who remained standing during all of this, the roar of excitement and exclamation continued for what seemed to me like over an hour, although it was hard for me to measure the time. For me, it was a timeless time. Still I watched the vision of Master Kirpal's eyes serenely surveying this happy chaos, while tears of gratitude flowed down my face.

When the ceremony was over, Master Darshan stood and spoke to the people in Hindi. I don't know whether anyone in the audience could hear him above the continuing roar of approval. After some closing formalities, the wet Indians, still standing, swept toward the dais in an overwhelming burst of affection. The wet Westerners, who had been sitting in front, quickly retreated to the sides of the tent in fear of being trampled. I was sitting on the ground close to the front and center and was not fast enough. I felt so nearly out-of-body that I was unable to stand up. I wondered if I would be crushed in the stampede of joyous Indians, but I was so intoxicated that I hardly cared. Somehow, I was unharmed. The vision of Master Kirpal's eyes and face in Sant Darshan Singh's body remained before me until the Master was hidden completely by the Indian devotees. I felt elated. Surpassing my hopes, the Master himself, or the Master "overhead" had indeed found a dramatic way to show himself to me. I was now confident that the same spirit that made Sant Kirpal Singh so special to me now resided in Sant Darshan Singh.

A few minutes later, when I asked a friend whether he had also seen Master Darshan's face changing, he replied "no" and seemed surprised by my question. Months later, I looked at a series of photos that had been taken throughout the turban ceremony: they clearly portrayed only Master Darshan throughout. So his face had not changed physically. I take it that my experience was something just for me—a visionary experience, a divine gift. The third and last day of the gathering was a celebration of divinity—of God's gift to us of this unbroken line of spiritual teachers who were awakening the spiritual consciousness in their initiates.

THE FIRST INITIATION

Master Darshan had not yet publicly initiated anyone, although many had begged for this gift. He said he did not want to stir up more controversy, but we knew he would have to begin initiating sometime. Twenty-three Westerners, most of whom had traveled with our group, came in the hope of receiving initiation. A week after the bhandara, they boarded a bus that took them to a private home where the first group initiation was to take place. I was one of the few "old" initiates invited, with the understanding that I would take photos. I felt very privileged to be present at this important group initiation.

As Master Darshan started giving the initiation instructions, a hush fell on the clamor of Indian street life outside the open windows, or so it seemed to me. The chirping of the birds was almost the only sound I remember hearing from outside for the next several hours. I felt the same charged atmosphere as I had many times before when Sant Kirpal Singh gave initiation. After the meditation, the great majority of those being initiated reported clear experiences of inner vision. Then, after the sitting for the listening practice, one man said he had been unable to concentrate on the inner Sound Current because he had been so captivated by the person playing the flute outside the window. The Master smiled and asked how many others had heard someone playing the flute. No one had. What this man had heard, it became clear, was the Inner Music of the flute, as the stories of the great Hindu deity Krishna made famous. Our friend sitting for initiation had had a lovely experience of the inner Sound without knowing it. The Master then asked those who had not had satisfactory experiences to meditate again. He wouldn't stop helping them until they were satisfied.

A meal was served afterwards, and everyone was jovial. Master Darshan touched his forehead and looked up. "It is all Master's grace," he said, referring to the Master Power overhead and appearing to be as impressed and grateful as the rest of us were. I was beside myself with joy at this happy meal, and couldn't bring my attention to any physical tasks. When photographing the Master and his wife together, I made mistake after mistake. Embarrassed, I asked them to pose over and over again, but the Master patiently laughed. Pointing at me, he said to the group, "He is in ecstasy!"

I had not only experienced the vision of the eyes and face of Master Kirpal in the face of Sant Darshan Singh, but had also confirmed the new Master through the criteria I had written down during my flight to India: the Master's humility, his ability to give darshan, his life being an example of the teachings, and finally, at the initiation ceremony, the ability to awaken inner experience in others. This skeptical questioner felt completely satisfied.

Dance, O my soul, with streaming eyes;
You have found the one you seek.
The heart overflows with gratitude;
It is no wonder that you weep.

CHAPTER TEN

A Frolic with Master Darshan[14]

1979

In 1977, while visiting a meditation center in Virginia, I met Heidi, a young lady who was full of life and who shared my spiritual interests. She, too, was an initiate of Master Kirpal. A few months later we were married. Then, in 1979 we made our first trip to India together. At that time, it was my hobby to photograph Master Darshan, and my interest was becoming known among the aspirants, because I had been distributing sets of slides made from the photos that might be used in our spiritual gatherings.

The very day Heidi and I arrived at Kirpal Ashram in Delhi, Master Darshan swept us away for a picnic at the Buddha Gardens, a beautiful park, filled with beds of flowers and manicured lawns. The gardens were built, he said, in honor of the 2500th anniversary of the Buddha's attaining nirvana. There, the Master treated us to a feast of laughter and photo opportunities. We were twenty or so young Westerners and about fifteen Indians, including the Master's family. As we walked into the park, which was many acres in extent, the Master's wife, Bibi Harbajan Kaur, whom we called "Auntie Ji," told Heidi and me, "This has all been arranged because of your visit, and you will take some good snaps."

Then the Master asked me, "Where do you want me to stand?You can command anything and I will obey!" Of course I did no such thing, but I did take many candid photographs in the beautiful setting, as did several other photographers.

The Master began distributing *prashad* (blessed food), pieces of the Indian sweet called *burfi*. When he came to me, he handed me a second piece, saying, "And one for your camera!" Then, everyone else with cameras got seconds too. When he came to Richie Seader and his large video camera, he had changed to distributing *ras gulla* (sweet Indian cheese balls). Richie didn't have a hand free, so the Master, smiling, popped the ball right into Richie's mouth. It was the size of a ping-pong ball. But it was the second one, "for the camera," that was almost too much for him. Everyone laughed in sympathy. I don't know how he managed to swallow.

Someone gave the Master a glass of milk to drink, but some of it dribbled onto his beard. The photographers put their cameras down out of courtesy, waiting until someone brought the Master a napkin. But the Master said, "Photograph it! The milk of human kindness is flowing out of every pore of man—even onto the beard!"

The Master walked to the food table, which was piled high with oranges, and asked, "Who would like to go out for some passes?" Most of the young men jogged out to the place where the Master was pointing, nearly fifty yards away. Then the Master made vigorous underhand throws, sending the oranges arcing through the air for the men to chase and catch. A few of the oranges hit the ground and shattered from the force of the throw. Laughing, he declared, "At a hundred yards, I can place the ball within inches!" Then he said he could "pop anyone on the nose with an orange, if that person isn't in a jolly mood. So, having warned you, I will not take responsibility for any broken noses!"

After this playfulness, we all sat down, and the Master gave an informal talk on the spiritual awakening among the youth in the West. The horizon-to-horizon flowerbeds offered a beautiful setting for all this. Then, of course, there was plenty of delicious food. When we left the park at dusk, Auntie Ji asked Heidi, "Well, did you like it?"

Before taking us to the garden, he had given us a tour of the new ashram, and after the picnic he sat with us Westerners for hours more, discussing various arrangements that might be made on his next US tour. Around ten o'clock that evening, the Master had a *sevadar* (a person giving volunteer service in the Master's name) take Heidi and me in a "three-wheeler" (a small, open taxi) to our lodging. Although we rode in this man's business vehicle, he refused to take any money. "It is Master's work," he said.

That was the end of our first day with Master Darshan. He took our breath away.

No rush there was to begin my lessons.
Time was given for joy and play.
A brief time was given: one day.

CHAPTER ELEVEN

Serious Humor[15]

1979

When Heidi and I visited Sant Darshan Singh for two weeks in 1979, we had a chance to see the newly established Kirpal Ashram in Delhi, India. The land had been cleared and a few old buildings cleaned for the use of the Master and his guests. A large courtyard had been paved with bricks for the weekly satsang meetings. The Master and his wife had just moved into a simple apartment on the second floor of one of the old buildings. Some Indian sevadars lived in some of the most dilapidated buildings, and a few guests from America and Europe occupied an old eight-sided guesthouse, which was picturesque but decaying. Some of the Westerners were lodged in a modern house a few miles away, which was being rented by the Master's staff. Heidi and I were given a room in the rented house. Only some twenty Westerners were visiting at the time, and we had a rare opportunity for close contact with the Master. I took many photographs, which were later distributed as a set of slides called *Stories of Love*. These are some highlights of our visit.

TOURING THE ASHRAM

News of the new Kirpal Ashram had traveled to the initiates all around the world, and Heidi and I were looking forward to seeing it. On our first day there I met Master Darshan as he stepped out of the room that he used as an office. I asked him if he would give me a tour of the grounds so I could photograph him in the new setting. He answered, "Yes, surely! I came out just for that."

He led me through the entire grounds and buildings, telling me some of their history. He showed me the tenting being erected for the upcoming bhandara for Hazur Baba Sawan Singh. While he explained these things, he spoke directly to me, with eyes so piercing I got lost in them. It was hard to concentrate on what he was saying about the ashram, what to speak of taking photos. After this he took us to the Buddha Gardens (see previous chapter).

PHOTO ALBUMS

The next day he showed us some photo albums of his activities during his recent US tour. They had been photographed by Santok Kochar of Chicago, and they were a pleasure to look at. Then the Master, making a serious request in his amusing and self-deprecating way, said that he would enjoy such albums even more if the photographers opened with a picture of Hazur Baba Sawan Singh, and then a picture of Sant Kirpal Singh. He explained that they had come before him, and it was their mission he was continuing. "And after that," he said, referring to the photos of himself, "you may put in any trash you like." He was telling me how to make future slide sets for distribution, but so humorously, so softly, that even as fiercely independent as I felt, still I was happy to follow his instructions.

THE BIRD

One evening the Master asked the Westerners to assemble in the meditation room, saying he would come and speak with us. While we waited, all sitting cross-legged on the floor, a bird flew in through the open window, as they frequently did. But a blade of the whirling ceiling fan struck the bird, and it fell onto an empty sofa, dazed. When someone tried to pick it up, it hopped away and fell to the floor, where it ran for several feet, stopping at the very place where the Master was to sit when he came. Perhaps we all had the same thought, that the bird was there to meet the Master, so we left it alone after that, trying not to frighten it further. The bird stayed there for some fifteen minutes, although people were sitting only two feet away. When the Master approached, the bird hopped into a corner of the room. The Master sat down and gently called to it. It hopped back, close to him. The Master offered it some water in a little dish, then tossed a few pieces of puffed rice prashad onto the floor. The bird picked up one piece of prashad in its beak, and, still holding the prashad, it hopped out of the room. Then the Master opened his talk by saying that all the animals of the earth might be our friends if they did not need to fear that they would be killed or caged. I never learned whether the bird regained the use of its wings.

A MEETING WITH THE ARCHITECTS

Late one evening, as Heidi and I were retiring at our quarters, we received a phone message that Master Darshan was going to hold a meeting to look over plans for the construction of new buildings at Kirpal Ashram. Would we like to attend? Of course we would! This meeting was to become a lesson for me in democratic decision-making. Heidi and I joined a group of about eight others, including the Master and two architects, both of whom were initiates, each of whom had separately designed a house for the Master, to be built at the ashram. This, they both did out of love, without compensation. First, the Master asked one of the architects to explain the whole site plan with all the proposed buildings. Then we were shown the two plans for the Master's residence. Both plans were for large houses, with two floors and many special-purpose rooms, for the Master, his family, his staff, and meeting rooms for the many visitors who came to meet with him. The business before us this night was to make a decision between these two plans. At least one of the two plans would be eliminated during this meeting, relegating a large piece of work to the scrap heap. Feelings might be hurt, something that Master Darshan was particularly sensitive to. Although this was to be his own residence, the Master asked the group to make the decision between the two plans, and he commented only occasionally.

One of the plans had the footprint of a large plus sign. This structure had a small central core with four wings on each floor. Each wing had a central corridor with rooms on either side, and all the rooms had windows. Each wing also had its own special purpose, and was divided into smaller areas, such as meeting rooms, administrative offices, and utility areas. Upstairs were mostly bedrooms. The ground floor was organized somewhat like an office building. I felt that this rational, hierarchical organization was excellent, being relatively easy for visitors to understand and navigate.

The ground floor of the other plan was more difficult to understand. Some of the rooms had fixed purposes, while others did not. Rooms were interconnected by doorways and hallways, seemingly randomly. Some rooms had no windows. I was reminded of a maze with paths that returned on themselves. I didn't care for that plan.

As a residential remodeling contractor, I felt I knew something about house plans. As the discussion opened, almost as if he were responding to my very thoughts, the

Master asked for my opinion. I recommended the first plan, and gave my reasons. I felt that a debate between the two plans was the appropriate way for our meeting to arrive at its decision, so, wishing to be fair, I asked the architect of the other plan if he wanted to make a rebuttal and defend his plan. He said, "No." I didn't understand why he wouldn't debate, but later that evening I did learn why, as will be seen.

At this point, one of the architects, a young man, asked the Master a question that seemed to have no relevance to the matter at hand: he wanted to know about the derivation of the word *woman*. Perhaps making light of a past personal misfortune, he wondered aloud whether the first syllable had anything to do with *woe*. The Master might have known the answer to this question, but he sportingly accepted the question. He called for dictionaries and volumes of the Encyclopedia Britannica, passing the books to various members of the group, giving assignments to look up a word or subject and report on it. In this way, a light-hearted linguistic discussion ensued. The Master then wove ideas about the word *woman* in and out of the discussion of the house plans. Jumping between two subjects made for a bumpy work session, but it kept the group laughing. The Master was using his usual sense of humor. In this case, I thought he was using it to soften something, perhaps the let-down for the architect of whichever plan was not selected. Such sensitivity was a hallmark of this Master's personality. Clearly the Master was enjoying this discussion, as he was a scholar of languages. I can't report the details of this amusing linguistic discussion, as I was trying to ignore it, focusing instead on the two house plans.

During these years I was learning, on-the-job, how to perform the work of this spiritual organization in the way that the Master wished. He frequently tried to bring people together, people with complimentary knowledge and skills, but often with contrasting, even conflicting, points of view. Learning how to work together lovingly, without fighting, was the great challenge and the great opportunity of this volunteer work. Sometimes I felt stymied in my work, and while waiting for a chance to talk to the Master about it, I often would meet someone who took an interest in the problem I was experiencing, had ideas to overcome it, and sometimes was even willing to work with me. Then, I might no longer need the meeting with the Master that I was trying to have. Also, it would often happen that the Master, asking for volunteers, would bring a group together that included members who had been fighting with each other, and he would establish a new committee to help those people handle the work that had been the source of discord. In this way we learned to appreciate each other's abilities, make compromises, and overlook differences. People tended to cling to the Master, even to follow him around, or to stop him when he was passing by. He had to be able to talk to many people, and after informing them, comforting them, or organizing them, he needed to be able to move on to other work. This is how the Master worked, and work of this kind would be conducted within the house we were now considering. Which plan would best facilitate this work?

The more our group studied the plans, the more one of them began to appear superior, as it would give the Master the most flexibility to move about without being hindered or trapped in one place too long. The maze-like layout of the second plan would actually work to the Master's advantage. That was not the plan I had championed at first, and I acknowledged to the group that I had changed my mind. Only when all the participants were basically in agreement, did the Master sum up the decision with such clarity that no one could doubt what had been decided or why. His reasoning, in fact, went beyond the reasons that had been raised in the discussion. I realized he had a better grasp of the plans than we did. I wondered if he might just have given his reasoning at the outset and saved us all a lot of work. But if he had, I would have missed a valuable lesson in democratic group process, and one of the architects might have felt that his proposal had not received serious consideration. What I would have made into a debate, the Master, along with this group that had previous experience of working with him, instead made into a meeting embodying a selfless process, with each participant trying hard to arrive at a good understanding of each plan and how it might be used, and then making the decision on the basis of that understanding. No one in the group was pushing for his or her own idea. That's why the architect wouldn't debate or defend his plan, and that was what I needed to learn. The Master was demonstrating good administrative practices without being didactic. The meeting was over a little before dawn. The next time I visited India, some two years later, I found that this house had been built.

DEMOCRATIC DECISIONS

A letter arrived at the ashram, addressed to me, concerning a matter before the board of directors of the meditation center in Bowling Green, Virginia, associated with these spiritual teachers. The letter raised a question as to whether a simple majority could make a major financial decision for the board without full discussion. As a member of this board, I had my own opinion, but I wondered how the Master would see this question. So, with little comment, I showed him the letter. After reading it, he said, "A decision like this should be made by the entire board. And it shouldn't be by a simple majority, either. Even a single dissenting vote should be heard." Then he said, "I am a democrat." He told me he would have more to say about this later.

Late that evening, with more people present, he repeated his earlier comments and explained further how decisions had been made in his government office, where, until his recent retirement, he had been a deputy secretary, with supervisory responsibility for thousands of civil servants. He said to us, "I very seldom made important decisions by myself. I would gather all the people involved and hear each person's opinion. If there was a single dissenting opinion, that was heard and considered by the others. It sometimes happened that that person's opinion had such force as to sway all the others. It may have been something the others had not thought of. If it was not possible to gather these people for a decision, then it was done by circulation. Again, if there was any dissent, those views were circulated, and the people were asked to vote again. Of course, it may have happened that the vote remained the same—but then I would have the satisfaction that I had done my job, and the dissenting person had the satisfaction that his opinion had been considered."

GYANI JI

The next afternoon I went to the empty sitting room in the Master's apartment, just to write in my journal. The Master had invited me to do so. After a while the Master entered the room with an elderly Indian man whom he introduced to me as "B.S. Gyani Ji, the nearest neighbor to Sant Kirpal Singh at Sawan Ashram." The Master told me, "He was the only man to spend every night from midnight to 4:00 AM with the great Master [Kirpal] in his room." Master Darshan was very humble toward this man. He tried to touch the man's feet (a common gesture of respect in India), but Gyani Ji simultaneously reached for the Master's feet, and they succeeded only in clasping hands, nearly at floor level, and then embracing.

THE SINGERS

The Master then asked me to accompany him to another room where Auntie Ji was singing a hymn of Guru Nanak with Heidi and several other initiates in preparation for a public performance. It was a beautiful scene. The Master sat down and listened to the singing. I felt overwhelmed by the love that filled that room.

INSPECTING THE TENTS

After the singing, he invited the eight or so of us present to join him and Auntie Ji on a walk out into the satsang grounds, where preparations for the Sawan bhandara were still under way. First, he made an inspection tour of the tenting, an expanse of large, colorful awnings, laced together, supported by poles at each intersection, which now covered most of the big patio. The awnings were mismatched, some were fairly new, and some looked old or dirty. The Master seemed to be displeased with what he saw, and he needed to express his displeasure to the man whose seva job it was to supervise the work of the tenting contractor. But the Master had a unique way of expressing himself without hurting people's feelings. Speaking in English, he said to that man, "We are paying so heavily, and these [canvases] are not just second rate, but third rate, fourth rate, and fifth rate! These tents look like they came from the archaeological department!" After he amusingly wondered aloud, whether they came from the Sikh period or the Mughal period, he asked the sevadar, "What have you been doing all this time? The contractor should be made to understand that although this is a bhandara [death anniversary], it is not a sorrowful event. These tents look like they are in mourning themselves!" The sevadar, who was not laughing, pointed out that *some* of the canvases were in good shape. The Master replied, "Well then you may pay for those at the first-rate rate. But *these* you may pay for at the fourth-rate rate."

A day or two later, when the bhandara began, I noticed that all of the tenting had been replaced with new or nearly new canvas, all matching. Apparently the sevadar had done his job well. The Master, rather than criticizing the sevadar and making him feel worthless, had called him to higher service, letting him know that something more was needed from him, and he must rise to that challenge. I was impressed by the Master's administrative skill. And why had the Master carried on his conversation with the sevadar in English, rather than the usual Punjabi or Hindi? I felt it might be that he wanted the Westerners present to hear this example—this lesson—of masterful human delicacy.

Later, the Master watched while I was writing in my journal. Then he commented, "You are taking things down verbatim? You know, I mix in a lot of humor to soften what I say. I hope you will convey what I say in the right mood." So—it was not just the Westerners who were to get the Master's lesson about the tenting. It was specifically, and pointedly, the writer himself.

UNDER THE DAIS

After inspecting the tents, the Master walked over to the dais, which at that time was a large brick structure with a concrete top. There was a tiny window in one of the brick sides, and loud, raucous, Indian popular music floated out of it into the ashram's tranquil air. The Master walked over and peered into the window. With a little smile, he called his wife to his side, and they both stood looking into the window for another minute. Then the Master walked around to the rear of the dais where there was a door into a room inside the structure. He opened the door silently, and he and Auntie Ji entered. Curiosity drove me to do a little peeking. There sat the resident of the room, who must have been one of the staff persons at the ashram. He sat on his cot, cross legged, eyes closed, and he seemed to be entranced in the loud music. The Master stood and watched him for several more minutes. Then we heard the music shut off, and there was much laughter within.

The Master, who must have seen me peeking, called out to me, "Brother, come and join in the fun!" So I, too, entered the room and heard the Master gently chiding the man for trying to meditate to music. He told us how, many years ago, he had become fed up with the radio, had his own radio disconnected, and had given it to his housekeeper. Then, looking at me and pointing to the man's tape recorder with a chuckle, he said, "So here is this man, listening to the radio!" Then the Master began looking around the man's room with his eyes wide open in a mischievous expression. He said to me, "And look at what he has done with my photograph!" Hanging from the ceiling was a red paper mobile in the shape of a carousel with a paper awning over it, from which hung three paper horses and riders. One of the horses had a small photograph of Master Darshan's face pasted over the rider's head and body, so it looked like the face was riding the horse. Another horse carried a photo of Hazur Baba Sawan Singh, and the third presumably was intended for Master Kirpal, but the job was unfinished. The Master, always one to finish his tasks, had a laugh over that unfinished work too. I felt I had been drawn into a hearty friendship between these two. I thought that this might not have been the first time the Master had teased this man. But as always, there were lessons, obvious enough, embedded in his warm humor. When the Master left, the man also followed.

"I WAS THE GUILTY ONE"

On another day, when I was alone with Master Darshan in the ashram courtyard, something reminded the Master of a story from the earliest days of his mission. He said, "Then, there was not so much to give out as prashad [blessed gifts], so I would take anything from the shelves [at his home]. Auntie [his wife] questioned me, 'I had this and that on the shelf, and now it is gone!' Well," he said, hanging his head in mock distress, "I was the guilty one, and I had to explain. Then I told her, 'Whatever is within my reach, or my eyesight, you should not question if it disappears!' So there has been no question ever since." He was telling me something about the roles of married people in India, which, as a recently married man, was of interest to me.

TAKING A PHOTO

One day the idea struck my mind to take a picture of the Master having a private discussion with some aspirant with a larger-than-life photo of Master Kirpal in the background. The significance of the large photo was that nearly all the people coming to see Master Darshan at that time were initiates of Master Kirpal. The large photo would represent the continued loving presence of Master Kirpal in the hearts of both the new Master and the aspirant. A number of people were waiting in the Master's apartment for private interviews at the time, and I knew that such big photos were in the room where he conducted the interviews. I asked each of the waiting people if I could accompany him or her into the interview to photograph. As I had feared, they all felt it would be a distraction. Disappointed, I put my camera down. Suddenly, one of the ladies changed her mind and called me to come in with her. Without my saying anything, the Master seemed to understand why I was there and what I wanted. He gestured around to the large photos on the walls, giving me a choice of backgrounds. I pointed at one of them, and he sat on the floor exactly where I had visualized him sitting. The lady sat down opposite him, also exactly where she should be sitting. I asked them to go on with their interview, and *there* was the picture, just as I had seen it in my mind. I took two exposures and quietly left the room. It all felt like something planned and carried out by a higher power.

HUMILITY

One evening, the Master was speaking to the Westerners. As usual, everyone including the Master, sat cross-legged on the floor. He commented that often an aspirant can't bow to his Master without some false piety or selfishness in it. It may be that the aspirant wishes to resolve problems in his life, and he knows that by taking them to a Master they will be resolved. So there is some ulterior motive other than reverence for the divine power within the Master. He explained that the Masters approach this by not letting the aspirants bow to them. "Rather," he said, "*we* [Masters] bow to *them*: We can truly see the Master [the divine Power] in them, and it is a good example to them. That is how we [aspirants] get a start in humility."

During this talk the Master spoke so softly it was hard to hear, even in the small room. But there was such intensity in his voice that the people sat very still for over an hour, listening attentively. He held us that closely to his words.

Now the learning must begin,
But not in memory of mere words!
In this school kindness and gentleness are taught,
Performance of duty, remembrance of truth.
Here the lessons must reach the soul,
Get ingrained in the life and make a man whole.

CHAPTER TWELVE

How I Became an American

1978–1979

When I was an angry young man, growing up in America, I saw all the social sicknesses around me: materialism, racism, violence, and, behind it all, a pervasive, closed-minded ignorance driven by pride and fear. Perhaps I was troubled by these societal weaknesses because society is like a mirror to me—when I'm quite honest, I find similar dark corners lurking in my own self. These negative perceptions of society blinded me at that time to the many positive aspects of American society.

At the Unity of Man Conference with Master Kirpal in 1974, I had learned the principle of human unity on a deep level, seeing divinity in Master Kirpal, in myself, and in another man, as I reported in chapter 7. Although I felt I was a citizen of the world, it had never occurred to me that the principle of human unity applied also to my own country. Master Darshan changed this attitude of mine with a lesson of just one sentence. But before I could learn from him he had to catch my wayward attention, and he did this through getting me involved in a complex story, which I will relate.

TAKING A PHOTOGRAPH

In 1978, four years after Master Kirpal's passing, Master Darshan visited Chicago. My wife Heidi and I went there to be with him, and I took my camera. During one of the Master's talks, I sat in the audience with my camera beside me. Without warning, the intonation of his voice changed, becoming charged with deep feeling. His face, too, reflected a mood of reverie, as he seemed to remember some deeply moving experience. Suddenly I became alert. Feeling inwardly drawn, I picked up my camera, put on a telephoto lens, and walked toward the dais. Probably I was disturbing the program with my activity, but I couldn't help myself. Without flash, I took several pictures of the Master's face, then I returned to my seat. In a while the mood passed. Many other interesting things happened during this visit, and I photographed them too. This incident receded in my memory.

When the film was processed, Heidi was looking through the pictures, and she called my attention to one of them that had been taken during the Master's intense mood. The expression of reverie was recognizable. Just visible in the photo were tears in the Master's eyes. This picture expressed for me much of what spirituality was about. The picture quickly became a favorite with the initiates. We had thirty or forty high quality enlargements made to distribute to other aspirants.

Shortly after that, in 1979, Heidi and I had an opportunity to visit Master Darshan in India. This was the same trip I described in chapters 10 and 11. We learned that some copies of that photo had reached the ashram ahead of us, brought by one of our leaders, and that the Master had taken all of them for himself. He would distribute them only to a few people.

At the time, Sant Darshan Singh was becoming well

known in Indian literary circles for his poems in the Urdu language, which were based on his spiritual experiences. One day I approached him in the ashram courtyard where he was surrounded by a few other Westerners. He turned to me and began speaking about that photograph. He told me, "That picture puts the lie to one of my verses!" Then he recited the verse in Urdu and translated it into English for my benefit (a little differently than it was later published):

> *The desires of my heart have been murdered in cold blood*
> *a thousand times over,*
> *But no one has seen any moisture in my eye.*[16]

"I was thinking of my Master, Hazur Baba Sawan Singh Ji, when you took that," he said, in explanation of his profound mood and tears of love. Then he asked me not to distribute that photo. "It is too personal," he said. I told him we had just made many copies for that very purpose. He replied, "Well then, the mischief has been done. Please give me several more copies." So I was happy to learn that even though my efforts to take expressive photos had met with disapproval, still in some way, he, too, liked that photo!

Then, in his loving way, he told me, "Only you could have taken that picture." I puzzled over that remark. I knew there was nothing special about my photographic skills. Maybe he meant that only I could have stood there "in cold blood" taking a photograph when he was in such a transcendent mood.

A CONVERSATION WITH MASTER DARSHAN[17]

A few days later, when the Master and I were alone, he explained why he gave the photo to so few people. He said many people would not appreciate its sensitivity, and he would prefer that it not be used to "decorate a drawing room." Our talk gave me a rare glimpse into the Master's humanity. He was a tender person who had been compelled to move into a public position. His poetry too, even in English translation, speaks of his great sensitivity, even though, as is common in mystic poetry, the meanings are often veiled in metaphor, so only those readers with some similar experience can perceive the poem's full meaning.

During the same conversation, I thanked him for the opportunity to know him and learn from his example of loving humility. He denied any responsibility for my gain, and said it was the two Masters [Baba Sawan Singh and Sant Kirpal Singh] working overhead. He said, "I have seen how the mission has grown so much in such a short time. I was no place four or five years ago [when his mission began]."

I could not accept that Master Darshan "was no place" at the beginning of his mission. I argued, "I saw you with Master Kirpal at the Unity of Man Conference, and I saw the same love coming from your face."

"Well, that is the Masters," he said with a dismissive wave. He emphasized that *he* was only human. He spoke of his limitations and the simplicity of his life, saying that the divinity I perceived was "the Masters [overhead]."

Again, I refused to accept the Master's humble self-abasement, and I told him that although I might not reach the divinity, I prayed that I might become such a loving man as he was.

He replied, "That is the first step. Our Master often said so."

SIGNING THE PHOTOGRAPH

A day or two later I was alone again with the Master. He picked up one of the photos that I had taken and said that although he didn't normally autograph photos of himself, he would sign it for me. I was thrilled, and I watched intently as he opened his fountain pen and signed his name, *Darshan Singh*, in light blue ink. He had my full attention now, and I was ready to learn something.

Under his signature he wrote the date. I had always seen him write the date British style, day-month-year, but he dated his signature American style. Surprised, I commented on this. He said, "Yes, because you are an American."

You are an American. That was his one-sentence lesson, delivered so informally and just slipped into the flow of events. Those four words reverberated in my mind, jarring against my deep-seated bitterness toward American society. When the Masters' words reverberate in my mind it usually has some effect. In this case, just a few days later I was able to say, "Yes, I *am* an American, and with all our social ills I am one of us, and I'm glad of that. Together, we may overcome these ills." It was a turning point for me: out of bitterness, into love; out of rejection, into human unity. The spiritual Masters have the most delicate ways of touching one's sore spots.

THE ART OF WOOING

This whole chain of events had begun with the taking of a photo during Master Darshan's visit to Chicago in the previous year. He gave many talks during that visit, and one of them, a talk which I attended, inspired by a wedding the Master had just witnessed, was later published under the title "Eternal Spouse" in the book *Spiritual Awakening*. One sentence from that talk stood out in my mind. It didn't get into the book, but in his talk the Master asked, "Do you know the art of wooing?" That was what I learned from this talk: The Master was out to woo us, to win our love and, I think, to challenge us to woo that Power overhead in return. This is a love in which the Master takes nothing from the aspirant: I've seen the restraint with which these teachers act, but this love relationship between the Master and the aspirant serves as a stepping stone toward being one with oneself, one with humanity, and one with the Ocean of Love. In mystic literature this personal relationship is sometimes called "being caught in the tresses of the beloved," expressing the overwhelming attraction of the spiritual Master's love. I feel that the main point of the experiences I've been describing is that they were all part of this wooing process. Many years of association with these spiritual teachers have shown me that loving influence. I've been heavily exposed.

For most of my life I've wanted to be a spiritual thinker, a scientist of the heart. Sant Kirpal Singh Ji himself encouraged people to enter the subject of spirituality with a scientific attitude: to seek verification of the teachings through first-hand experience. But unexpectedly, I became caught in a love I could not have anticipated or imagined. Spiritual love is deeper than thought—deeper than science. And there's an excitement and magnetism in this love that speaks to me of life itself, of reality. Master Darshan made the seriousness of these teachings quite clear: he declared, "This is God's work. No man can do it. No man can stop it."

He had a one-sentence lesson for me,
Delivered so informally.
No longer could I poison my mind
With contempt and anger toward my kind.

"Just a transfusion," the doctor said,
As lifeblood was passed to the patient in bed.

CHAPTER THIRTEEN

A Bouquet on the Rooftop[18]

1979

In India it is often very hot during the day, but it cools in the evening, and people come onto their flat rooftops for a quiet time under the stars. Master Darshan's simple apartment had such a flat roof, surrounded by waist-high parapet walls. He often invited guests at the ashram to join him there for quiet gatherings, which sometimes lasted until dawn.

On this night, the neighborhood around Kirpal Ashram in the city of Old Delhi was quiet. Few sounds reached the high roof. Occasionally, watchmen walking the streets would bang their long walking-sticks on the pavement and blow their whistles softly. To the people sleeping in their homes, this was the sound of security. The effect from this distance was almost musical. Some forty or fifty spiritual aspirants sat together on the roof in a silence so deep that one could almost hear it. The balmy air and velvety darkness enclosed them all in a soft embrace. Occasionally, a teacup clinked delicately. Master Darshan, sitting among the devotees, spoke softly. The people strained to hear his words, which were spoken gently, quietly, as a lover speaks.

A more human love was on the minds of one American

couple who were there this night. They were engaged to be married and planned to have the ceremony the next day, in India, with Master Darshan in attendance. So the Master honored them with his attention and gave them his wishes for a happy marriage. He urged both of them to make their spiritual aspirations the centerpiece of their marriage, that both, together, should reach the divine goal.

A friend of the couple brought out a gift package, and Master Darshan formally presented it to the couple. When they opened it, they found it was a tea service, with teapot and cups. This suggested some imagery to the Master, who pointed out that the cup can be filled only if it is placed *below* the teapot, and that is how the spiritual aspirants should place themselves in relation to their spiritual teacher—then they will be filled with divine grace.

When, in the wee hours, the gathering seemed to be coming to an end, people stood to go, but they heard someone walking up the stairs to the roof. Soon the devotees saw the Master's gardener, an old man full of devotion for Master Darshan and Master Kirpal. Shyly, he stood at the head of the stairs with a bouquet of multicolored flowers in his hands, which he had evidently just cut from the ashram's gardens. Master Darshan walked over to him and took the flowers. Apparently, he had been expecting this delivery. Then the Master stood very still, removing one flower at a time from the bunch and putting it back, making his own arrangement. He did not look around, only at the flowers, for about five minutes. The aspirants, still standing, wondered about the meaning of this and watched in total silence. No one dared to move. People nearby could hear the Master humming very softly as he gave this long, loving attention to the flowers. Some were overcome with tears. At last, he turned to the couple, and handed the bouquet to the bride-to-be. As she took it to her heart, tears were streaming down her face.

Then, the Master walked down the stairs, leaving the aspirants in laughter and in tears.

Silent night, holy night,
I am just in awe tonight
That in this world of war and fear
Such a teacher could be near.

CHAPTER FOURTEEN

Covering for Us

1988

The spiritual Masters speak of how the aspirants are protected in many ways. The Masters are said to take over the karmic accounts of the aspirants, to wrap up their karma for their release from the lower planes. Many initiates tell stories of automotive accidents or roadside breakdowns in which they had been protected. As I look back on my work in Mississippi, I can see that protective hand over my head in many of my activities there, even before I was initiated, although I was unaware of that protection at the time. One can become so accustomed to such protection that it's easy to grow careless of one's safety, even though the Masters wish the aspirants to take some responsibility for their lives and safety. One can experience the protection of that Power overhead even in very small ways. Here is the story of Master Darshan "covering" for me when I made a minor, but very public mistake during one of his tour visits in the US.

The Master had asked me to present a slide show during one of the evening programs at the meditation center in Bowling Green, Virginia. As often happened, there was little time to prepare for this event, so I asked someone else to load the slides into the projector tray. The slides had to be loaded in a certain orientation, upside down, which was counterintuitive for an inexperienced person. I should have checked the tray to make sure the slides were all inserted correctly, but I did not.

At the evening slide show, with a packed audience of hundreds, all was going well until one slide, showing Master Darshan standing full length, head-to-foot, came on the screen upside down. This was disrespectful to the Master, and it was my fault. Immediately, Master Darshan, sitting in the audience, called for a microphone and asked that the upside down slide be left on the screen. While the microphone was being arranged and my mistake remained in front of the large audience, I had an opportunity to wonder what kind of criticism I was in for. But when the microphone reached the Master, he announced that this upside-down photo was not a mistake, but had been arranged on his orders so that all could see that "my head is at the feet of the Masters!" We all had a hearty laugh, and the slide show continued. It was a minor incident, but the memory remains clear to me as a reminder of the thoroughness of the Masters' protection and propensity to cover for us.

Being protected—in the palm of God's hand—
Finding time and again the sheltering grace:
One senses a link with the Power divine,
One becomes fearless in duty and service.

CHAPTER FIFTEEN

"A Master Surgeon of the Heart"

1988

In 1974, Master Kirpal held a human unity conference in India (chapter 7). As I've previously written, during that conference Master Kirpal demonstrated to me the divinity within himself, within another ordinary man, and much to my surprise, within myself. Then a command from the Master Power overhead told me to sit and think, because I was now ready to understand the meaning of "human unity." I quickly concluded that the divinity that had been shown me could be understood to exist in *all* humans, even if it was so deeply buried that it couldn't be seen, as it had been in me. This was a watershed experience, and from that time on it affected my relationship with other people, leading me to be more continuously conscious of the divine nature of individuals, gradually making me more respectful and compassionate than I had been before.

After this, the annual human unity conferences were passed from one organization to another around the world, and thirteen years later, in 1988, a human unity conference was to take place in Delhi. Master Darshan's mission and several other organizations were asked to cosponsor it. I was blessed to be present again.

Before the conference started, Master Darshan spoke to the Westerners who were attending. He told us that this series of conferences had lost much of the spiritual inspiration with which Master Kirpal had infused the original sessions in 1974. Even for me that inspiration was a distant memory. Indeed, most of my memories of Master Kirpal had become distant and vague. At this new conference, military, government, and religious leaders, including the Dalai Lama, spoke. This time the speeches were all in English, and it was apparent that political and economic planning—not spiritual understanding—was on most of the speakers' minds. I was surprised to learn that many of those present were unfamiliar with Master Kirpal, who had started it all.

Master Darshan inaugurated the conference with a reverent tribute to Master Kirpal. Humbly, Master Darshan lit an oil lamp before a large photograph of Master Kirpal, invoking his blessing upon the meeting and speaking of the spiritual oneness of humanity. Watching this, I felt my own buried memories of Master Kirpal awaken. This opening ceremony affected my heart so deeply that there must have been more going on beneath the surface than merely the lighting of a lamp and a few words spoken. Now, the message of human unity that Master Kirpal had made so alive to us in 1974 seemed to me to be the most important concept that needed to be expressed at this conference as well. In his inaugural address to this conference, Master Darshan said, "When any activity is being pursued over an extended period, it is necessary, from time to time, to recall the lofty vision and goals of those who pioneered it. . . . Thus the objective of our tribute is to rekindle the vision which inspired these conferences."[19]

And rekindle the vision he did! During this opening ceremony my memories of experiences with Master Kirpal flooded back into consciousness. At the same time I saw that most of the other participants in the conference hadn't had the benefit of Master Kirpal's powerful lesson: a lesson that had shown me the meaning of human unity at the spiritual level, which already exists at a level transcending matter and intellect. I wanted very much to help the people at this conference become aware of this deep reality. I was surprised to feel my heart going out to so many people, as normally I was socially withdrawn. Feeling more daring than usual, I wanted to say something to them on that subject. I mentioned my wish to Master Darshan, who encouraged me to give a short talk about it to the conference. He also asked the organizers to give me time in the program. The next day, I spoke to those people about learning of human unity from Master Kirpal through visionary firsthand experience. I made a distinction between intellectual solutions to human problems on the material level (which the speakers were pressing) and spiritual understandings that deeply affect the human heart. If we could all be continually conscious of the divine core of humanity, then the problems of poverty, war, and violence would be far less likely to arise. It was good to say these things, but even as I spoke, I felt that my words describing subtle things didn't begin to carry the weight of those Master Kirpal had spoken. He had made his life an example of human unity, and further, through his eyes, he gave the experience to those who were ready to receive it.

THE MASTER SURGEON

My new wish to share my understanding made me aware that something in my consciousness was growing. I was taking a step toward realizing the ideal of human unity and was experiencing the desire to give the loving service to whomever needed it, which naturally accompanies this awakening. But my renewed consciousness also awakened me to the ego and negativity festering within myself. I thought, "If I can see this sickness in myself, others might see it too." I felt ashamed. At the same time I could feel some movement in my heart that was abruptly changing me. It was a little frightening, and for a day or two I felt I was in pieces—I hardly knew myself. I was troubled by these changes and needed to understand what was happening to me.

At the busy ashram where I was living, I found a rooftop where I could be alone, and there I sat down to think it out. Quickly, my Master's subtle presence came close to me, speaking gently, as a kindly doctor might comfort a patient. I received his message sentence by sentence, slowly. At first came only the meanings, wordless: a message to soul, not to mind. Then, with mind grasping to understand, words also came:

> *You are in the hands of a Master Surgeon of the heart.*
> *This is open-heart surgery.*
> *It is that serious and that wonderful.*
> *When the operation is over, there will be no scar,*
> *and the cure will be so complete that no one will even remember the sickness.*

I thought, "Open-heart surgery!" That's the kind of wordplay these Masters relished, but that wasn't the way my own thoughts worked. So I became confident that those thoughts were a message from my Master, identified with that Power overhead. I felt that my quandary—needing to understand what was happening to me—was fully answered.

The words I received contain compressed meanings related to the Masters' spiritual teachings. Those words might need explanation here. My understanding of these meanings was received through thought transference, and I'm confident of my interpretation. The Master Surgeon was, of course, the Master overhead. He was a surgeon of the heart because his work was to "open" an aspirant's heart—the soul—to divine love, which once it had known but had now forgotten. The medical imagery was quite appropriate, as this was a cure for a disease—call it forgetfulness of divine love, or call it the illness of ego—it amounts to the same thing. It was "serious" in that opening the spiritual heart and removing the ego that blocks both human unity and inner spiritual growth is a life-or-death matter to the serious aspirant. The procedure for such surgery and the depth of its results are as breathtaking and "wonderful" as the latest advances in medical surgery. "When the operation is over" refers to the completion of the reconstruction of the soul's identity—specifically, the strengths and virtues developed during the "man-making" process and the soul's inner journey Homeward. Although the aspirant is a participant in this, it is the Master—overhead—that drives and steers this process. Since only the outer dross of the worldly attachment and ego is removed in the process, leaving the soul in its original pristine state, there can be "no scar" made in the divine surgery. Once cleansed, the soul shines with divine beauty. "No one will even remember the sickness" refers to people's—and even to God's—tendency to forgive and forget. When children, or even adults, turn away from bad behavior and begin behaving admirably, then those who know them tend to forget the past and respect them as they are at present. Even when that soul comes before God, its dark past can be forgiven and forgotten. Then the aspirant's position will be as if the sickness of ego had never occurred. When the soul comes to understand that it is not the individual person it had taken itself to be, but comes to identify itself with God, then the actions of the individual little self become unreal, and the soul awakens as from a troubling dream. The Masters explain that that is how they see the souls that come into their fold: they see a pristine soul, muddied as it might be, but just needing some cleaning up. They know that they have the ability to cleanse the soul and that its light will then shine out.

I later found that the "cure" was a long-term process, one that worked slowly over decades and continues in me to this day, so deep-seated is the illness of ego. That very hopeful message that I received could well be said for all the initiates of true spiritual Masters, as initiation represents the Master's acceptance of responsibility for a soul's restoration. As fortunate as I have been in my association with these spiritual teachers, my case is really no different from the many others who receive initiation in this spiritual hospital. Spiritual teachers say that in time, all the initiates will experience that cure. I say my case is no different, but also I've seen that each of the initiates is different, with unique backgrounds and needs, and each has a different path of spiritual education that unfolds in unique and interesting stories.

For thirteen years following the passing of Sant Kirpal Singh, I had avoided the pain of bereavement that would come from his remembrance. Master Darshan had made that avoidance easy for me with the warm, accepting hand he extended. But now, at this human unity conference, he had awakened my memories, and I found myself able to bear my heart-wound, the "half-drawn arrow," (chapter 9) and even to value it. As I began remembering my own Master Kirpal, a deep love and gladness began to fill my heart. I felt he had been within me all along. As I thought of him, I felt his divine love within, as if he were glad that I was back with him, without any suggestion of admonishment for my absence, which was understood as what I had needed to go through.

Even while writing about these experiences, my thoughts are directed to that Master Power within, and I have a sweet sense of that presence in my consciousness, even the sense that it is not just me writing. Those initiated on the spiritual path often express an awareness of no longer being alone, of having an inner companion on the way, and that's my experience too. Often this presence is so immediate that I can't contain the tears of gratitude. How subtle is the influence of these great teachers!

On my last day in India, I told Master Darshan how my

memories of Sant Kirpal Singh and his teachings had been so awakened during the conference, resulting in my Master's presence and his message. Master Darshan smiled warmly and replied, "That was my only purpose."

Both of my teachers were poets
Who loved to play with words.
So I knew where the message came from,
One spirit encompassed them both.

Here's a message of hope for soul and mind:
That my case was under the care
Of One who was able to take the soul
Back to the Home that was lost.

CHAPTER SIXTEEN

"I Have Built a Son"

1988

Sometimes events seem to be unrelated, and yet in time they come together, revealing an unseen guiding hand. The events described in his chapter are like that.

On the first day of the 1988 Human Unity Conference in Delhi, Sant Darshan Singh Ji was sitting on the stage at the speakers' table, and I was sitting in the audience. He cast his glance on me, and our eyes formed a bridge. He didn't turn away, but kept looking at me. Then his face transformed into another face, almost as if his own face had become transparent, with another, different face gradually appearing behind it. I was reminded of my visionary experience thirteen years previously when his face seemed to become that of Master Kirpal (chapter 9). But this face was quite different.

Then another man at the speakers' table spoke to the Master. Clearly, this man hadn't seen any change in the Master's face. Master Darshan turned his attention away from me to speak to this man, and in my perception his face returned to normal.

When his conversation with the other man was over, he turned back to me and reestablished the bridge from eye to eye. Again, the new face appeared. I felt attracted to this face, a strong face, much younger than Master Darshan's, with flowing beard and powerful, direct eyes. This person seemed to take an interest in me. At first I wondered if this was the face of a Master who had initiated me in a previous life. This exhilarating play of the Master's eyes continued for perhaps twenty minutes—or so it seemed in that timeless time, until the meeting broke for lunch. We exchanged no words, and I didn't ask Master Darshan about the significance of this experience. I felt energized, joyful, and very focused afterwards. Months later I was to find even more meaning in it, which I will explain shortly.

During the conference and at satsangs, Master Darshan nearly always had his son Rajinder with him. Once, at a different gathering, a satsang, when no one else was with him on the dais, he asked his son to come and join him on the dais. Rajinder seemed hesitant, but when the Master insisted, he climbed the steps, and humbly, he sat down cross-legged at the extreme rear of the large, nearly empty, dais.

When it came time for me to return to the United States, Master Darshan called me into his office. He served me refreshments and gave me several gifts. He seemed to be searching for things to give me and to be having trouble finding suitable things. I was thrilled when, almost apologetically, he handed me the typescript he had used for his talks at the conference. He wasn't asking me to do anything with it; it was a gift for remembrance. I read that precious typescript through several times on the long flight home to help me cling tightly to my inner connection with the Master overhead, even in the stressful environment of the long flight.

Before Master Darshan said goodbye to me, he brought up a new subject: Thinking, perhaps, of his visit five years earlier to my house, which I had been building with my own hands at the time, he spoke of his new residence at the ashram, in which we were sitting, the same house whose planning was discussed in chapter 11. He told me that he did not own this house: the ashram property was managed by a board of trustees, to whom he paid rent, "and it's quite a bit of money, too." Then, still on the subject of houses, he said, "My associates in government service have built houses with their incomes, and now they are very well off. I haven't built any houses."

Then he looked at me pointedly and said, "But I *have* built a son." I understood immediately—by thought transference as I take it—that he was telling me that his son Rajinder had reached the spiritual goal. I wondered why he would say such a personal thing to me, but I remained silent.

I didn't know it then, but this was to be my last meeting with Master Darshan. Six months later the Master passed away. At last I understood: without causing me any worry for the present, he had, without my knowing it, communicated to me what I would soon need to know—that I could look to Sant Rajinder Singh as a spiritual Master.

Later, when I saw Master Rajinder on the dais, in his new role as the Master, I again saw visions of the strong face that Master Darshan had showed me. I now realized that the face that had appeared with Master's Darshan's face at the Human Unity Conference in Delhi had been that of Master Rajinder, but I hadn't recognized this at the time because, in that vision, his beard was long and flowing, whereas I had never seen him without his beard bound up under his chin. And beyond that, in the vision his eyes were full of power, such as I had never seen them radiate. I saw this vision in the face of Master Rajinder on many occasions in the years that followed. Finally, I asked Master Rajinder to explain the meaning of these visions. He replied, "Sometimes a disciple is given such an experience so he can be confident he is on the right path." Once that understanding was locked in my heart, those visions seemed no longer necessary, and they stopped. I found it very interesting and reassuring to experience how, with delicacy and foresight, these spiritual teachers can convey needed information and assurance to their aspirants, with sensitive regard for the aspirants' feelings or fears.

To be taught through visions!
Who would have thought it could be?
The death of my loving teacher
Is too momentous for words,
Too disturbing to know in advance.

The fearless soul could understand;
The fear-ridden mind could not.
So soul was prepared for the change
Through a glimpse of what was to come.

PART 4

Years with Sant Rajinder Singh Ji

CHAPTER SEVENTEEN

"The Spring Night of Separation"

1989

Master Darshan passed away on May 30, 1989. I arrived at the airport in Delhi at 1:00 a.m. local time, less than forty-eight hours later, on the same plane as the first wave of initiates from America and Europe. I was still numb from the news and had not begun to deal with my grief. I knew that the staff people at Kirpal Ashram would be in as much shock as I was, and I didn't expect anyone to meet us at the airport, as they usually did. So it was quite a surprise to see the welcoming face of Raghubir, an initiate who worked at the airport, waiting for us. Not only was he there to greet us with a sweet smile, but he had chartered a bus to take us to the ashram. It was astounding to me, just as it has been every time I've visited the Masters in India, to feel I was being welcomed into a loving family. I felt I had come home, even though Kirpal Ashram would seem terribly empty without Master Darshan.

When we arrived at the ashram, around 3:30 AM, we were led to a room in the Master's residence where Sant Darshan Singh's body lay on a platform surrounded by flowers and large tubs of ice. It was a heart-wrenching sight. While we numbly stood there, the Master's wife, Mata Harbhajan

Kaur, entered the room. Her face looked ashen. She quietly greeted us visitors, then walked to the Master's body and bowed her head, touching her forehead to the Master's chest. She stroked his beard gently with her fingertips, and shook him gently as if to awaken him. She spoke a few words in Punjabi as if speaking to the Master. I didn't ask her what she said; this was too serious an occasion. Years later, when I read her memoir in English, I found that she too had found this moment significant enough to speak of it in writing. She had said to the Master, "Please stand up and greet everyone. Your children have come!"[20]

A room nearby had been arranged for meditation and contemplation. Most of us went there to sit after viewing the Master's body. It was in this house that Master Darshan had told me, "I haven't built any houses. But I *have* built a son" (previous chapter). The significance of this, almost his parting words to me, was now fully apparent: I knew that his son, now Master Rajinder, must assume the role of the new spiritual teacher. I had many other sweet memories of Master Darshan in this house. Remembering these things, my heart swelled with love and renewed grief.

Before long, the first hint of dawn touched the sky and whole flocks of birds began to sing in the trees just outside the residence. The night was nearly over. As the sky grew light, the group I had arrived with was led to our quarters. The men were to be housed, dormitory style, in the "glass house," a solarium atop the building that the Master and his wife had used as their residence in the days just after the ashram was established. I felt a new wave of love and grief, thinking of the wonderful nights I had spent with Master Darshan on this very rooftop. The story I call "A Bouquet on the Rooftop" (chapter 13) had taken place here.

That afternoon, Master Darshan's sons, Master Rajinder and his brother, were to arrive in Delhi from the United States. Many of us went to the airport to meet them. I still remember the first sight of Master Rajinder as he entered the reception area where we waited. His face was solemn but composed. When he saw all of us waiting for him, his face became wracked with the grief that we shared, and a single sob escaped from him. He embraced many of those who were there.

That evening Master Rajinder met with the Westerners in the Master's residence and explained to us many of the Sikh funeral traditions that would be followed, in which we would be invited to participate. It amazed me that he had the composure to recognize the needs of the Westerners and to assist us so quickly.

MASTER DARSHAN'S CREMATION

The funeral ceremonies began the next day. The Master's body was brought from his residence and placed high on the back of a truck arrayed as a float, laden with flowers. Master Darshan's body was dressed in white with an ivory colored turban, as he had dressed since assuming the role of the Master.

A huge crowd of Indians waited outside the ashram gates. When the float passed out into the Delhi streets, everyone could see the Master's body, and there was a new, loud, communal gasp and outpouring of grief.

It was several miles to the cremation grounds. The weather was sunny and hot, nearly one hundred degrees Fahrenheit. The Westerners had been invited to ride in the vehicles in the procession. I accepted the ride, but some chose to walk the whole distance in the street with the Indians. As the procession slowly moved through the city, more and more people joined it. I had a good view from a seat high on top of a truck leading the procession. From there, I could take photographs, and when we passed through a large square, I saw many thousands of people following the Master's body. They filled the square, and there may have been many more on side streets that I couldn't see. It seemed that the whole city had come out to pay reverence to this great spiritual teacher who had lived among them.

At the cremation grounds, devotees carried the Master's body to the top of a high ceremonial platform. In this writing I have only occasionally used the word "devotees," because of its intimacy, but here it must be used, as this handling of the Master's body was truly an act of devotion. In India, cremations normally take place outdoors, in the open. His body was laid on top of a low pile of firewood. Flammable melted *ghee* (Indian clarified butter) was poured over the body, and the devotees dropped thousands of rose petals over it, symbolizing our love for him. Then more firewood was placed all around and on top of the body until it was completely hidden from view. I was told that the firewood being used was sandalwood, a fragrant and costly material. Devotees helped to build this pyre. I was surprised to find how much it meant to me to sprinkle a few handfuls of the flower petals and place several pieces of the firewood, while many others did the same, in some last little symbolic service to the Master whom I had loved so much. Finally, more *ghee* was poured over the logs.

Master Rajinder lit the fire, and the fuel-soaked logs quickly ignited, sending hot flames high in the air. The heat became fierce on top of the platform, and the people had to retreat down the steps for their lives. I wondered why I was bothering to escape from the heat, as my life felt valueless without the Master. But a thought came to me that I was not to die now—although there was no explanation of why.

I watched the flames burn for perhaps an hour, then, seeing the devotees leaving, I walked toward the vehicles. On the truck that had carried the Master's body, men with ice picks were breaking up the large cakes of ice that had kept the body cool. They were giving the pieces of ice to the crowd of devotees, who sucked on it as a kind of blessed prashad. It was a welcome treat in this hot weather. I wanted some of this ice too, as I was faint with the heat of the day, and I felt it would be something from the Master. One of those men must have seen my desire, and he waved me over to himself, holding out a piece of ice as big as a fist. His eyes were sparkling with love. I gratefully accepted the ice in both hands, the traditional way to accept prashad. But I had been told that commercial ice in India was particularly unsafe as drinking water, and these men seemed to give no thought to sanitation. I hesitated. Then I thought, "This is *prashad*," and I need not concern myself with its physical condition. So I, too, sucked on the ice. Then the thought came to me to just lean my head back and hold the ice on my forehead. I felt that that thought was a message from the Master overhead. When I did as suggested, the cold water ran over my hot face, and the blessed coolness quickly descended through my whole body. It was a delicious sensation. From the standpoint of physics, I don't think that the amount of cooling I experienced was actually possible. I think it was, indeed, something from the Master. The funeral pyre must have burned well into the night, but I went back to the ashram.

The next day we returned to the cremation grounds. All that remained of the funeral pyre was a bed of glowing embers. These were now extinguished with water. I watched and photographed while Master Rajinder, his brother Bawa, and other family members performed the ceremony of sifting the ashes for fragments of bone. These fragments (called "flowers" in this ceremony) were washed in a mixture of water and milk, with delicate flower blooms floating on top (jasmine, I think). Closely watching Master Rajinder's facial expressions during this ceremony, I saw that the death of his father was an unimaginably deep loss to him. When this task was complete, the "flowers" were deposited in an urn, which was wrapped with saffron cloth. Master Rajinder symbolically placed the urn on top of his turbaned head and carried it down the steps of the platform, back to the ashram. For days, devotees from distant parts of India filed through the Master's residence at the ashram to view the urn of bone fragments and say their own farewells to beloved Master Darshan.

REMEMBERING MASTER DARSHAN

In satsang a few days later, Master Rajinder spoke words of solace both in Hindi and in English. Now that the new Master was presenting satsang, the ashram seemed to be getting back to a normal mode of activity. Just one sentence that Master Rajinder uttered stands out in my memory: "Whatever memories we have of Sant Darshan Singh Ji Maharaj must be sufficient to last for the rest of our lives." I had a wealth of memories of Master Darshan. Still, as so many of us feel when a dear friend dies, I wished I had even more such memories.

During this time it was announced that a book of English translations of some of Master Darshan's poems, along with a commentary, on which he had been working during his final days, was nearly complete and would be published soon. It was to be entitled *Love at Every Step*. This title, a quotation from one of his verses describing one of his early mystic experiences in meditation, also described for me the Master's life itself, and thinking of this I felt joy as the sharpness of grief subsided.

If the death of Sant Kirpal Singh fifteen years before had left me with a wound, a "half-drawn arrow," I now had two such wounds. But having drunk this bitter cup of grief to the dregs, I was quite surprised to find at the bottom only sweetness. In this world the pain of separation seems to be an integral part of love. I learned during these days that grieving may be very hard, but there is no reason to fear it. When the object of grief is spiritual, there may even be great joy hidden in it. Perhaps this grief, which causes such focused attention on the divine, can even accelerate the aspirant's progress.

Eleven years later, in 2000, I would again experience deep personal grief, though of a different kind, when my wife, Heidi, died from cancer. My understanding of the spiritual teachings helped me grasp that at her death she had merely relinquished her physical body, and that the life of her more real, conscious soul would continue on higher planes, in more cheerful surroundings.

After Master Darshan's cremation, thoughts of home became uppermost in my mind. I was troubled about a family crisis that I had left unresolved. Master Rajinder took an hour of his time to discuss my family problems with me, apparently bringing his full attention to it, as if nothing else were happening. While I was alone with him, I asked what news I could convey to the initiates back home concerning successorship. I spoke of my fear of a repetition of the controversy that arose after the death of Sant Kirpal Singh. He replied that it would be up to the board of directors at the ashram to make the announcement, and that they had not yet met, as it was too early in the grieving process, so I should not speak of it. "But," he said, "we feel the transition will go smoothly this time." And it did.

After this discussion, I felt I should return home as quickly as possible. Friends at the ashram helped me move my flight reservation to the next day, and I left India, having been there less than a week. The funeral continued without me: The Master's ashes were carried to the River Ganges at the town of Rishikesh, a place of sacred pilgrimage. There, the ashes were carried out to deep water in boats and were consigned to the river with further ceremonies. In a Sikh tradition, no part of the cremated body was kept. Remembrance was to be a purely internal thing.

Within a few weeks, the book *Love at Every Step* was available, and a few months later, Master Darshan's wife, Mata

Harbajan Kaur, published a recording, singing many of the poems in this book. It was the first time she had recorded songs in English for distribution. I used to play this recording in my truck as I drove around the Washington, DC area, going to various job assignments. The poems were thoughts that arose from the Master's period of discipleship. One of these poems described his feelings of painful separation from his own Master, Hazur Baba Sawan Singh Ji. Now, one of his poems especially, described our feelings of separation from him. Mata Ji sang these words in a sweet voice expressing the poignancy of love and the pain of separation. Sometimes, while listening to this song, I would have to pull my truck to the side of the road while my heart and eyes overflowed again. Mata Ji sang:

The spring night of separation becomes more tearful as it advances,
And my remembrance of you tosses ceaselessly in the bed.

When your devotee's condition alters but a little,
Life presents itself to me with another cup of sorrow.

Your remembrance is sewn to the hem of my heart;
No matter where I go, I cannot forget my sorrow.

The spring is in full bloom and is most inviting, but without you, O Beloved, every flower is on fire.
It is as though each moment I were being stabbed with pain.

The intensity of love melts life itself;
It is a candle, O Darshan, which is consumed by its own flame.[21]

—DARSHAN

CHAPTER EIGHTEEN

Two Windows on Love

1999

At an Easter gathering of initiates in the Chicago area, Sant Rajinder Singh talked about darshan. He asked, "What happens during satsang?" He answered: From the outside (the level of the senses) it appears that little happens: the people are sitting, the Master may be speaking, he is looking around, and that's about all. But from the inside, much more is happening: When the Master's eyes connect with another person's, the language of love may be spoken eye-to-eye, heart-to-heart. No one but the Master and the aspirant know what has transpired. For the aspirant, the experience is fascinating, riveting, and deeply fulfilling. This is darshan, the Master's sharing of who he is and what the aspirant can become. Words are truly inadequate to describe the lessons of spirituality, but experiences such as darshan convey far more than words. Master Darshan made many metaphoric references to darshan in his poetry. Of his verses that have been translated into English, one of the best known describes darshan from the aspirant's viewpoint:

The moth was speechless, and the flame was silent;
In the entire assembly there were only two who shared this secret.[22]

This verse uses a favorite image in mystic poetry, that of the moth (symbolizing the aspirant) and the flame (symbolizing the spiritual Master) and the wish of the aspirant to fly into the luminous eyes of the Master, losing his individual identity, trading his lesser life for a much larger, divine identity. The "assembly" is the satsang, the gathering of aspirants in the presence of the Master—like the gathering in Chicago that I was describing—and the "two" are the Master and the aspirant, so focused on each other that no one else is present within that communion. The "two" are sharing the "secret" of divine love from the Master, something so delicate, so vulnerable, so indescribable, that it's considered to be "secret."

One of the unique characteristics of a spiritual Master is the great love that he bears, just beneath the surface, which a receptive aspirant might glimpse during darshan and occasionally in other circumstances too. At this gathering, one of these rare glimpses was about to occur for all those present, both through darshan and through more conventional seeing.

When Master Rajinder finished his discourse, the program coordinators announced that Mr. Harbans Singh would sing a *bhajan*, a devotional song, in this case a song based on a poem by Master Darshan. Mr. Singh stepped to the podium and began to sing the bhajan. He was unaccompanied, but his slow, sonorous voice conveyed a deep solemnity. Since the words were in an Indian language, and the audience consisted mostly of Westerners, few present understood the words, but something of its solemn mood did convey. While Mr. Singh continued his solo, the Master's eyes turned from one aspirant to another. It was an opportunity for darshan.

Suddenly, the Master looked away from the audience, put his hand over his eyes, and bowed his head. His shoulders began to heave. All could see that he was weeping silently. He picked up a tissue from beneath his armrest and wiped his eyes. Those watching must have wondered what led to this abrupt and unusual change in his mood. The explanation was probably that he was reacting to the words of the bhajan, which he understood, although the Westerners did not.

The Master raised his face, seeming to regain control, only to dissolve in tears once more. As the slow, somber song continued, the Master made use of tissue after tissue. This went on for ten minutes or more. It was difficult for the aspirants to watch their dear teacher be so overcome, but these aspirants understood from their own experiences that such tears came from an inner upwelling of love. Sharp pain and great sweetness come together in such tears. But it remained a mystery what words had led to his tears. Tears are contagious, and the aspirants, in sympathy, shed many more tears that evening.

When the bhajan was over, the Master regained his composure and the program continued. From the dais, the Master asked the program coordinators to set up the equipment for a video, scheduled to be the next item in the program. As assistants moved the equipment into place, the Master began explaining the words of the bhajan. He began, "This bhajan was about the death of Master Kirpal." At once, the initiates knew what had led to the Master's tears. Master Rajinder was both grandson and spiritual student of Master Kirpal. Also, many of those present were students of Master Kirpal and had experienced their own grief at his death. But Master Rajinder got no further than this. At the name of his Master, he dissolved into tears again, and more tissues appeared. He said no more about the bhajan, but the initiates had all the information they needed. The Master asked the program coordinators to start the video.

All those present had shared a sweet and revealing glimpse of the Ocean of Love that resides just beneath the surface of such spiritual teachers. That glimpse was conveyed through both darshan and the Master's tears: two windows on love. It was a reminder of the reality and the depth of the spiritual love that is so alive within them and that is gradually being awakened within the hearts of the aspirants.

> *My love for my teachers gives a road to my goal.*
> *The one I'm attached to will be my companion*
> *Far above and beyond my earth-bound mind.*
> *I must follow.*

CHAPTER NINETEEN

Receptivity

2006–2016

With the passing of Sant Darshan Singh Ji and the emergence of Sant Rajinder Singh Ji, my spiritual education also changed. Whereas Master Darshan had treated me like a kindly father or indulgent elder brother, the new spiritual Master treated me more as a fellow worker within our organization, and he had expectations of me. I quickly realized that my time as a child on the spiritual path was over, and that I had now to stand on my own feet, to behave in a manner that reflected the spiritual teachings, and, through my own life, demonstrate what spiritual living meant for the many people being attracted to this new teacher. I had to do some fast growing, but I had been well prepared.

I found that there were needs in the group whose meetings I attended, so, working with several other older members, we did our best to meet those needs. Occasionally I conducted some of our meetings, and I became convinced that a need for organizational information going out to our membership was important, so, with our teacher's encouragement, I started a monthly newsletter, printed and mailed, shortly before the days of electronic communication. I continued as its editor for eight years. This was all volunteer service, as was all the work done in our organization, including that of our spiritual teachers.

When I retired from my construction work in 2006, I moved from the Washington, DC, area to Bowling Green, Virginia, where I built my retirement home. For many years I had been associated with the meditation center located there, dedicated to our spiritual teachers, and I had been a member of the board of directors ever since the center was formally established. I had many friends there, and my wife, son, and I had visited nearly every month. After my wife died I began to think about retiring from the work I did for my livelihood. I considered selling the home I had built near Washington, DC, and building a new home in a simpler rural setting. Increasing my service in our organization was not in my thoughts. Then, during a visit to Bowling Green, I realized that many of my friends were there, and it would be a pleasant place in which to live. At the time, I felt that I was being shown these facts by the Master overhead, with the suggestion that I might retire there, and the neighborhood of the meditation center then seemed like a desirable place to retire. So, I moved to Bowling Green and built a new home with no stairs, in which I might grow old.

Shortly after I arrived, a new management committee was established, and the center's director asked one other local resident and me to join her to form this new committee. I was happy to join, as I enjoyed working with both of the other members. But within a few years, due to attrition in the small committee, I was left with a personal responsibility for the center. Bit by bit I established new functions that I thought would serve the purpose of the center. I followed what I felt were promptings by the Master overhead. But I lacked confidence in my receptivity, and I thought I might be doing something that the Master wouldn't approve of, or was failing to do something that he might expect of me. Ever since I began pursuing spirituality I've struggled to sense the difference between thoughts of my own mind and promptings from the Master overhead. This was especially difficult when my own wishes were in conflict with the promptings, and I was unable to bring the two into agreement. From past experience I knew how valuable it was to review such things with Sant Rajinder Singh Ji. As a start, in 2016 I wrote a long letter outlining my administrative activities and asking all the questions that were on my mind. Shortly after that, I visited him in Chicago, attending one of the large gatherings there, and he agreed to meet with me.

Our meeting took place in a suite in a hotel. When I entered the Master's suite, I found him in an armchair before a low table in a sitting area. An assistant showed me where I might leave my coat and other items that I carried with me. Whenever I meet with the Master, I'm always very conscious of how valuable his time is, so I was trying to be efficient, stowing my things. But the Master was just sitting quietly, watching me, and when I was ready he motioned me to another armchair nearby. I gave him a copy of my letter, which I think he had already read but apparently didn't have with him. He quickly scanned through it and then began answering all my questions, one after the other. I took brief notes as he spoke. To my gratification, all the things that I had established at the meditation center were approved, which gave me new confidence in my receptivity and the feeling that even in the future I might better trust myself to understand what was needed.

There was only one thing the Master didn't approve: I had wanted to conduct seminars at the center on literature from other religions and other branches of Sant Mat. Some of these writings, having parallels to our teachings, were quite interesting to me, and I wanted to share them with others to demonstrate the universality of the spiritual teachings and to share my enjoyment of the unique ways in which they were expressed. But I felt that this might not be approved as a formal activity of the center. I had been advised to that effect by others, so I had not held such seminars yet at the center. I thought this might be an example of a conflict between my own wishes and the promptings from "overhead." I was right: the Master asked me not to hold those seminars. He explained that only by basing my seminars on the published writings or videos of the Masters could we be assured of dealing with truth. In the months that followed I complied with his instructions in this matter, and I've been surprised at how much the aspirants enjoyed the seminars. Here again, my intuitions were confirmed as to the Master's preferences, this time in a matter that went against my own wishes. I have a hope to learn to offer selfless service in the Masters' mission. What's challenging is not performing the service itself but performing it selflessly. This time I had to learn to put aside my own fond wishes. That should have come as no surprise to me: in 1979, as I described in chapter 12, Master Darshan had recited to me his own Urdu verse, with this impromptu translation:

The desires of my heart have been murdered in cold blood
a thousand times over,
But no one has seen any moisture in my eye.[23]

I hadn't realized it at that time, but Master Darshan had been describing to me a principle that I would need to understand some twenty years later. It was a principle that the spiritual Masters follow in their own lives: that the work of this mission was more important than themselves. Now, I understood the principle that the work of the spiritual mission is more important than any individual's wishes, *including my own.*

During my meeting with our teacher in Chicago, another challenge rose to my mind: I had a wish to ask some personal questions, unrelated to the meditation center. But a thought came to me that this interview had been granted because it had to do with meditation center business, and my personal interests were not really appropriate here. I thought this was a prompting from the Master. Here was the same principle challenging me again! I'm sure that if I had asked my personal questions, the Master would courteously have answered them without criticizing me, but again this was a matter of receptivity. I followed the prompting that I received and did not ask those questions. I was glad when another prompting quickly came, saying that I had done the right thing. These thoughts and promptings went through my mind even as the Master and I were speaking together without pausing. And later, my personal questions resolved themselves without my lifting a finger. Years later, I still feel that if I had yielded to the wish to ask my personal questions, it would have to some extent diminished the selflessness of the service I wished to provide to the meditation center.

As I reflect back on these insights, I feel led to the thought that perhaps *most* considerations of myself are secondary or even irrelevant in my life, and that thoughts of service and of the Higher Power are the *only* matters that should concern me. While this was a new thought to me, Master Darshan's much higher thinking had already expressed that conclusion in one of his verses: "*The aim of my life is to continually and completely sacrifice myself.*"[24] I have never heard the Masters ask the aspirants to make such a sacrifice, but the Masters are our exemplars of how a true devotee lives. We see them perpetually giving of themselves in service to others. So here is another exalted goal I find placed before me that I could pursue at the meditation center or in all parts of daily life, if I were able. I think that this may be something to grow into over time, as part of spiritual maturation.

How can one tell the difference between messages from the divine and messages from the mind? That can be difficult, but in some cases there is enough information to make the distinction. For example, when inspirational ideas came to me during the writing of these pages, I would take the new text and try to insert it into what had already been written. Sometimes it wouldn't fit: perhaps the existing text was clearer than the new, or the new text was tangential to the subject at hand, taking the writing in an unwanted direction. I didn't use those messages; I took them to be only mental ideas that might be useful or not. But in other cases the new text fit well, helped to clarify a difficult subject, and—perhaps the most telling criterion of all—the new words seemed so sweet, so truthful, that tears came to my eyes. These messages I took to be from the divine.

In making that distinction, I don't mean to denigrate the mind, whose work I value. Over the years my mind has slowly, incrementally, come into better alignment with my spiritual aspirations, to some extent becoming a "friend," as Master Kirpal had suggested it might (chapter 5), as its willingness to work toward spiritual goals and receive inner promptings has grown. Even the mind, with its limitations, is a creation of God. But I still take my mind to be a somewhat irresponsible friend. I'm in no position to relax my vigilance. I'm taking only the first baby steps in this subtle discipline of receptivity.

Master Kirpal asked his aspirants to develop the skill of receptivity, so that we could benefit from that wisdom within and act with wisdom in our service to others. But it was decades after his death before I had a good sense of what that skill really was. Such things come only in their own time, and it's only in old age that I'm becoming more receptive to a kind and wise friend within. My intellectual approach to life made a barrier that kept this friend at a distance. I was seeking reality, and I think my rationalism helped for a time. But developing an acquaintance with the Power within required transcending rationalism. As Master Kirpal has said, "Reasoning is the help and reasoning is the bar as well."[25] But transcending rationalism doesn't mean giving free rein to the emotions. It means living and learning at the level of soul, as I've attempted to illustrate in my own learning experiences. At the level of soul emotions will still express themselves, sometimes strongly, but they don't rule the aspirant. Learning at the level of soul brings its own confidence to the search for reality that even the rational mind can't equal.

During my interview with Sant Rajinder Singh, when he came to the end of my list of questions, having answered them all, I thanked him, and he smiled and gave me a loving look. Having received darshan and still being conscious of the high value of the Master's time, I stood and went to pick up my coat and personal items from the other corner of the room. I thought that while I did this, another person waiting for an interview might be walking in, and the Master's attention would be turning to him or her. When I had all my items together in my arms, I turned for a last glance toward the Master. He was still sitting alone, and he was watching me. His eyes were overflowing with love. Across the room, I received a second and far deeper darshan. That glance of love embraced me and lifted my spirits high. That darshan was the pinnacle of my visit and a highlight of my life.

The watchdog was cautious:
"O David, check your ego.
Just measure your little step
Against the distance still to go!"

But the student was grateful:
"Still, a small step is a step,
And the eyes of the reverend teacher were
Smiling."

PART 5

Reflections

CHAPTER TWENTY

The Challenge of the Mind

For many years I've tried to become a person worthy of the spiritual teachings and the abundant grace that has been offered to me. Why would I put so much effort into something that might lead only to a swollen ego? Spiritual teachers say that if one wishes to become able to meditate deeply, then the mental faculty associated with a soul—the mind—must be clean. This is the lesson that I learned at my very first face-to-face meeting with Sant Kirpal Singh (chapter 6): I learned that love itself in pure selfless form called me to be equally pure, and I didn't have that purity. I wasn't ready to meet that love, and I withdrew from the spiritual love in his eyes through my own volition. Most of my life since then has been dedicated to the "man-making" process, as my first teacher called it. The spiritual teachings say that it is only when the aspirant becomes pure—becomes truly human—that he or she can meditate deeply. Conversely, they also say that one cannot complete the man-making process until one learns to meditate deeply! That's necessary so that baser pleasures that are relinquished through mental discipline can be replaced with deeper pleasures of a higher nature. The upshot is that both disciplines go together, reciprocally: both man-making and meditation must be practiced together in the life of the spiritual aspirant.

When one sits down to meditate, in a quiet place, with meditation instructions fresh in his mind, with intent to focus on inner Light and maintain simran—the repetition of the charged names of God given to the aspirant at initiation, the first challenge he experiences is his own mental life opening to his consciousness. What a field of thought is presented! The existence of such thoughts might have been unsuspected, and the thoughts might be unwanted or unworthy of the aspirant: lustful, egotistical, or violent ideas. The thoughts might be negative or positive: inventions might be suggested, or seemingly profound understandings be offered. In spiritual meditation the mind must be quiet before the divine can be experienced. Few people are able to create this quiet space in their meditations through their own efforts. In meditation, one learns where his mind will go as soon as the anchoring effect of normal physical life is removed. My experience is that within minutes, the aspirant might forget his intention of meditation and be drawn into the flow of the mind. It's no wonder that the aspirant is taught to discipline his mind. If he is to meditate spiritually, then the aspirant has to learn another way to anchor the mind.

I've experienced all the mental challenges that I just described, and still the decisive resolve needed to quiet the mind eludes me. My spiritual teachers have not been hesitant in suggesting ways to bring about that mental stillness. The single most powerful technique they give is that of simran—the repetition of the charged names that can be practiced at any time of day when mental effort isn't needed in one's work. Its use helps to build new habits of sustained concentration; especially, it trains the mind to stay away from negative thoughts.

In spiritual meditation, a strong anchor such as simran is essential. That is the new anchor for the mind when the physical world is left behind. The mind is likely to resent this practice, insisting on its right to unfettered freedom. The mind tells one that he (the mind) is who we are, that it is wrong to restrict him. That is what he said to me. The mind knows little about the soul and doesn't understand that the soul, not the mind, is the center of consciousness. So the challenge is before me to gently, respectfully, bring the mind around to seeing the advantage in being self-disciplined. It will take time. I pray for and anticipate help from the spiritual Power overhead.

There are times when the mind accepts and even embraces spiritual discipline. After long meditation sessions, when one is especially relaxed, one might experience a sweet calm, a lightness of being, suggesting the possibility of further progress into higher consciousness. I take such experiences as a premonition, a promise, of greater consciousness to come, and so I believe I'm on track toward that goal. I'm an intellectually oriented person who values a life of ease. I've never practiced any form of yoga or mental disciplines for spiritual purposes other than what I learned from my spiritual teachers, at least not in this life. I don't expect myself to soar suddenly into the beyond, but I would like to make incremental progress in the spiritual direction.

I'm attracted to this path of meditation in part because I wish to verify, in my own experience, the remarkable visions of those who have had near-death experiences, who report some taste, some foreknowledge, of the death process—for most an ecstatic experience in which they lose all fear of death. A few say that even after their near-death experience, they could return to a blissful state of near-death consciousness through meditation. Spiritual teachers confirm that possibility. But if, as I've experienced, the mind can become undisciplined without the anchor of physical consciousness, then some fear of death might be justified, although problems with the mind's lack of discipline are seldom reported in the near-death accounts that I've seen. Is that because near-death experiencers are simply having mental illusions without knowing it? I'd like to know the truth of it through my own experience.

According to the spiritual teachers, exploring the death process while still living in the body would be only an elementary stage of meditation. They promise that as meditation deepens, one can also explore the whole world of mental phenomena, from emotional states, to the causal web of life, in which the complex interconnectedness of living entities can be understood. Even the all-knowing "universal mind," the home of the individual mind, can be accessed: the end goal of yogic practices, I have been told. Beyond that are purely spiritual regions, in which the soul transcends the mind and ego (individual selfhood), and meets the Creator from which it emerged, coming to her own home, becoming one with the divine, described as the ultimate goal of the spiritual quest. These things are mostly beyond my imagination. Perhaps, in time—or beyond time—I, too, might explore these purely spiritual regions.

The student recedes in meditation
To a quiet place where calm invites
The soul to desert the heavy body
And rise above in cosmic flight.

The student sees a distant fire
Of self-oblivion bright.
Will the student spread his wings
And fly into that Light?

CHAPTER TWENTY-ONE

Gratitude

Once I visited Master Darshan in India when many Western aspirants were there. The Master called us together for a brief lecture. Apparently some people had been complaining to him about the injustice and hardships of life—a familiar theme among my acquaintances in the West. The Master, seeing from the perspective of the law of karma, which suggests that there is no such thing as injustice, asked us to consider things from a higher perspective. He told us that such an attitude expressed ingratitude toward God, as we all had so much to be grateful for. First, he said, we have been blessed by a birth in the human body, the only body in which it is possible to make substantial spiritual progress. He asked us to consider the millions of members of millions of lower species, and calculate the odds against being granted a human body for this incarnation! Second, he explained, we were fortunate against all odds again to find a spiritual teacher who had the ability to guide the soul back to its Home. Third, we have been accepted into that teacher's school through his initiation. With some effort and dedication on our parts, we all had the opportunity to transcend into higher regions. How could we possibly feel shortchanged? How could we possibly not feel gratitude? (The Master used the word "we," including himself as one of the aspirants.) That lecture found its mark in my heart, and since then I've found more and more reasons to be grateful. A grateful life is a happy life, still another reason for gratitude.

What happens as the ego—the little self—diminishes? Does one grow smaller? My answer is: no. One does grow more relaxed, more willing to let things be as they are, to let others do as they see fit to learn whatever lessons they need in life. In this way, one's forceful footprint in the world might lessen, but one's kindness, one's loving presence, one's wish to be of help to others increases, so that one might even have more influence to awaken kindness in others. As the ego diminishes, the presence of the divine grows, becoming more integrated in the personality. That *expands* the identity of the aspirant to larger fields of consciousness. The person no longer feels that he or she is the doer of his actions. The divine spirit within becomes the doer. That's the very essence of the spiritual learning process. It's a transition in identity. I've heard my first spiritual teacher, Sant Kirpal Singh Ji Maharaj say, "I never dream that I am the doer." He described himself as "nobody; I am Mr. Zero," and yet he was an immense personality! He was too honest a person to engage in false humility. So what was he? I can only conclude that, having completed the process of the spiritual path, he *was* that humble Power overhead. And he was teaching his students to become that too. What a teacher! What a school! I'm grateful for my exposure to this spiritual school.

In this school I've experienced being treated by the teachers with the respect that might be given to someone who is at least potentially able to rise to that level of vision. That means I was respected as a human being should be respected. I've experienced the respect and love that could only be expressed by someone with divine vision. If only I could be receptive to that teaching, to that love! If only I could rise to that level myself. I *must* rise to that level! Through self-imposed challenges such as that, I'm being encouraged to take one step at a time in this learning process. This is an education that is warm and friendly, insistent and exacting.

I'm also grateful for the help in everyday life extended by that Power overheard. It has come to my aid in moments of crisis, such as dangers to body or to property and in emergencies on the road far from home when sometimes crises were resolved before I could even think of what I might do.

While I'm counting my blessings, a big one is the contact with inner Light and Sound that is given to the spiritual initiates. When the initiated aspirant turns his attention to that inner experience, calmly, with love, he can experience those manifestations of the divine Power. He can be reminded that he is connected to a higher source and can enjoy its love. He can carry his happiness with him even when his meditation is over.

That Consciousness overhead also has aided me in the writing of these pages. Often this help comes as I slowly awaken mornings, not yet oriented to the world, with mind and body relaxed and receptive to words and thoughts that come to mind. I reach for paper and pen to write them down. Those ideas become interwoven with my own thoughts and expressive preferences, so that finally even I can't easily distinguish between the words of the author overhead and those of the writer on earth. Sometimes I wish that this divine conversation in the form of a writing partnership might go on forever. I think that this memoir would not have been written at all without that inner partnership. That helper knows far more than I do, and he added a great deal of his own thought to these pages. He takes no credit for his many contributions. Can anyone wonder at my gratitude!

My life of spiritual study has been a scientific experiment in the sense that I embraced what I thought was of value and lived accordingly as best I could. It is said that at the end of life, each human soul undergoes a life review from an elevated perspective, evaluating her life choices. From that, the soul learns something definite: soul knowledge, which may become so much a part of our own character that it can guide future life choices, leading eventually to fulfillment of life's purpose.

Does my experiment in spiritual living prove anything to other people? Probably not much, as I can't convey the actual experiences, only descriptions in rough words. That's okay, since we are all in school together in this earth plane, performing laboratory science: we make our own hypotheses with the values we choose, knowingly or unknowingly, and we perform our own lab work by living out the consequences of our choices, whether or not our choices were wise. From our own observations during life or in our life review, we learn which choices were of value and which were harmful—at the level of soul—which we might or might not remember intellectually. We will be at least a little wiser in our next incarnation. So, even with its inherent pains and frustrations, experience in the laboratory of life is a great blessing.

I've always valued helping others to learn things when I'm able to do so. I've taught chemistry and physics in high school, demonstrated construction techniques for my employees, and conducted a "freedom school." But in my role in our meditation center, I've found that the most effective ways to teach are by modeling behaviors, leading group discussions, telling stories, asking questions for discussion, and by sharing my own (sometimes embarrassing) learning experiences. I've discovered that through my preparations and interactions with the participants in our study sessions, I learn a lot as well. I encourage the participants to bring up their own questions, even if they challenge our spiritual teachings. I have no fear of challenging questions, not even though I sometimes have to admit that "This question is over my head." We're friends sitting together to help one another understand the teachings at an intellectual level. I don't attempt to change people's religious beliefs. People from many different cultural and religious backgrounds attend our programs, and I respect those backgrounds that give them an intellectual scaffolding from which to explore the spiritual teachings. In spirituality, the important thing is to learn to meditate and to develop a personal relationship with the divine, however the divine might be conceived. Spirituality isn't a somber subject; we have fun with it and laugh together. I love helping others to understand this subject.

This book you're reading: is it an aspect of my teaching compulsion? My purpose has been primarily to tell the personal story of my spiritual education, but yes, I hope also to convey some challenging ideas, especially the concept that human consciousness has far more wonderful potentials than is usually assumed.

PUBLISHING

I've long felt that the spiritual Power overhead was giving me extensive help in writing this story about my spiritual education. Perhaps that Power had a story of his own to convey. For that reason, I couldn't think of this writing as just my personal property. I felt that my current spiritual teacher, Sant Rajinder Singh Ji, should have some say in whether, or when, or in what form, this book might be published. A message came to me within, saying, "Go ahead and publish." But I thought that because publication is something that I desired so much, if this were a trick of the mind, then I might easily fall for it. Again, that message came. Again, I would not trust it. At last, I had an opportunity to present a draft of the book to our teacher when, in December 2022, I visited him in Chicago. As I approached him, that inner message to go ahead and publish came even one more time. Still, I would not trust it. So I told the Master that I was hoping for his advice and consent about publication. I thought that he would need to read through the book before replying, which, considering his workload, might take many months. But he simply responded that he had read a previous version (which I had mailed to him years before), that "those were sweet stories," and that I should "go ahead and publish." His words agreed completely with the messages that I wouldn't trust. Not only could I proceed with publication, but I was given a new assurance that I could—cautiously—trust the messages within.

THE FINAL EXAMINATION

My first spiritual teacher, Master Kirpal, once said that when the end of life approaches, the spiritual student takes the lessons much more seriously. Using metaphor, he said, "When the time of the final examination grows near, the student takes his book even to the bathroom!" At the age of 80, I have finally begun to take the inevitability of death seriously and to worry whether I will be able to pass my own "final examination." I take Master Kirpal's metaphor of the "final examination" to signify that a student has gained sufficient understanding and detachment from the world that he is able to leave his body on his own before death or at least be able to relinquish the body easily, naturally, at the time of death. The Master might also have been referring to facing the life review without anxiety. He promised that the disciplined initiate will not have to face judgement by the "angel of death," but that the Master himself will guide the soul into the beyond, giving any counsel necessary.

During a conversation with Master Rajinder, I wanted to express my anxiety about dying, so I resorted to Master Kirpal's metaphor and told him that I was "worried about my final examination." It took him just half a second to grasp the unspoken meaning behind my statement. Then his face expressed surprise and concern that I should be worried at all. Quickly, spontaneously, he reached out and took my hand in his, patting it and stroking it while saying, "I think you'll do fine." But the gesture with his hands expressed even more than his words: I felt he was answering my metaphor with a nonverbal metaphor, meaning: "Don't worry; I've got you safely in my hands. I love you." And that was God speaking.

This was very similar to the message that I received many years ago, when the message was more formally expressed as, "You are in the hands of a Master Surgeon of the heart" (chapter 15). I can hardly express the relief and gratitude that I felt upon receiving this new assurance that I would not face death in lonely solitude within, that he would see to it that I was prepared, and that as Master Kirpal had once said, death would be "a loving change."

To deeply respect one's spiritual teacher,
While being treated by that teacher
As one worthy of respect—
What more could a student ask!

With gifts of understanding
Layered over understanding,
Mind grows content and quiet.
What more could a student ask!

To find that one's own teacher
Is the essence of the goal
Of his spiritual education—
What more could a student ask!

To learn that the student in his soul
Is of that essence sanctified:
That he's divine in nature too—
What more could a student ask!

REFERENCES

1 Hazur Baba Sawan Singh, "Be Free Forever," part II, *Sat Sandesh* 19, no. 8 (July 1986): 17 (quoting *Adi Granth*, Raag Maaroo, M. 1, p. 1009.)

2 Stephen G. Cary et. al., *Speak Truth to Power* (American Friends Service Committee, March 2, 1955), https://perma.cc/NP4J-6LUL.

3 *Merriam-Webster Dictionary*, s.v. "behaviorism," accessed September 25, 2021, https://perma.cc/H3RH-J4BB.

4 Kirpal Singh, *Man! Know Thyself* (Lisle, IL: Sawan Kirpal Publications, 1992), 7.

5 William Shakespeare, *The Tragedy of Hamlet, Prince of Denmark*, ed. Barbara A. Mowat and Paul Werstine (Washington, DC: Folger Shakespeare Library, n.d.) 1.3. 84, accessed June 10, 2022, https://perma.cc/2ZNG-L2KQ.

6 Loose translation of a Hindi caption on a published photo of Sant Kirpal Singh in the writer's keeping: *paramātmā ko pānā mushkil nahīṅ / insān kā bannā mushkil hai.*

7 Kirpal Singh, *The Night Is a Jungle* (Tilton, NH: The Sant Bani Press, 1975), 155.

8 "The Augean Stables," Hercules: Greece's Greatest Hero, Perseus Digital Library, last modified September

2, 2008, accessed September 25, 2021, https://perma.cc/6MZK-M5ST.

9 Kabir, *The Ocean of Love: The "Anurāg Sāgar" of Kabir*, trans. Raj Kumar Bagga et. al. (Sanbornton, NH: Sant Bani Ashram, 1982).

10 Parts of this chapter are based on letters from the writer to family members.

11 Kirpal Singh, "The Remodeling of Our Destiny," *Sat Sandesh* 7, no. 3 (March 1974): 9, https://perma.cc/UQN9-6YV6.

12 Kirpal Singh, "The President's Concluding Remarks," *Sat Sandesh* 7, no. 3 (March 1974): 32, https://perma.cc/UQN9-6YV6.

13 From here to the end of the chapter, the text is based on David Edmonston, untitled journal, August 17–30, 1975 (handwritten unpublished manuscript, hereafter cited as Edmonston Journal).

14 This chapter is based on Edmonston Journal, April 28, 1979.

15 Edmonston Journal, April 28–May 10, 1979.

16 Impromptu translation given by Sant Darshan Singh, quoted from Edmonston Journal, May 7, 1979. The published translation is in Darshan Singh, *A Tear and a Star* (Lisle, IL: Sawan Kirpal Publications, 1998), 39.

17 This section is based on Edmonston Journal, May 10, 1979.

18 Edmonston Journal, May 3, 1979.

19 From the typescript given to the writer as prashad, described in chapter 16.

20 Harbhajan Kaur, *Nourished by Divine Love* (Lisle, IL: Sawan Kirpal Publications, 1998), 187.

21 Darshan Singh, *Love at Every Step: My Concept of Poetry (Lisle, IL: Sawan Kirpal Publications, 1989), 50.*

22 Darshan Singh, 56.

23 Repetition of the verse in note 16.

24 Sant Rajinder Singh, quoting Sant Darshan Singh, in *Satsang Themes*, vol. 4a, "Difficulties in Developing Devotion," segment 1 (Lisle, IL: Science of Spirituality, 2002) (internal educational material).

25 Kirpal Singh, *Jap Ji: The Message of Guru Nanak* (Lisle, IL: Sawan Kirpal Publications, 2011), 85.

www.ingramcontent.com/pod-product-compliance
Lightning Source LLC
LaVergne TN
LVHW050956080826
845145LV00009B/2321

* 9 7 8 1 9 6 0 0 9 0 2 2 5 *